# The Ultimate Coffee Cookbook

365 Days of Flavorful & Easy Homemade Coffee Recipes to Become a Home Barista in No-Time. Creative Ideas to Prepare the Perfect Brew for Every Occasion

### BY

### David M. Roastery

© Copyright 2023 - All rights reserved.

It is not legal to reproduce, duplicate, or transmit any part of this document in either electronic means or printed format. Recording of this publication is strictly prohibited and any storage of this document is not allowed unless with written permission from the publisher except for the use of brief quotations in a book review.

# TABLE OF CONTENTS

**Introduction** ———————————————————————————— 5

**Chapter 1: The Great Variety of Coffee** ——————————————— 7

   The Many Types of Coffee ———————————————————— 7
   Differences in Flavor ——————————————————————— 9
   The Allure of Fragrance —————————————————————— 11

**Chapter 2: From Harvesting to Roasting** ——————————————— 14

   Harvesting Coffee Cherries ————————————————————— 14
   Processing Coffee Beans —————————————————————— 16
   Roasting Coffee Beans ——————————————————————— 18

**Chapter 3: It's Not Just About Coffee** ————————————————— 20

   Moisture Content and Temperature —————————————————— 20
   Deciphering Coffee Labels ————————————————————— 21
   Personal Preferences and Experimentation —————————————— 22
   The Art of Brewing ———————————————————————— 23

**Chapter 4: Equipment Tips** ———————————————————————— 25

   Espresso (Moka) Machine —————————————————————— 25
   Pour-Over Devices: Melitta, Chemex, Hario V60, Kalita Wave ——————— 26
   French Press ———————————————————————————— 28
   Aeropress ————————————————————————————— 29
   Siphon (Vacuum Pot) ———————————————————————— 30

**Chapter 5: Perfecting Your Coffee Brewing Skills** ——————————— 32

**Chapter 6: Tricks and Mistakes to Avoid** ——————————————— 35

   Tips and Tricks for Making Successful Coffee ———————————— 35
   Mistakes to Avoid and How to Remedy Them ————————————— 36

# Chapter 7: Coffee Recipes Around the World ———————————— 39

Espresso Martini ————————— 40
Turkish Coffee ————————— 41
Ethiopian Coffee Ceremony ————— 42
French Vanilla Latte ——————— 43
Italian Hazelnut Espresso ————— 44
Moroccan Spiced Coffee —————— 45
Greek Honey Frappé ——————— 48
Cuban Café Con Miel ——————— 49
Italian Affogato ————————— 50
Indian Filter Coffee ———————— 51
Moroccan Mint Coffee ——————— 52
Chinese Yuenyeung ———————— 53
French Café au Lait ———————— 54
Spanish Cortado ————————— 55
Mexican Café de Olla ——————— 56
Irish Coffee ——————————— 57
South Korean Dalgona Coffee ———— 58
Finnish Kaffeost ————————— 59
Jamaican Blue Mountain Coffee ——— 60
Malaysian Ipoh White Coffee ———— 61
Russian Coffee with Vodka ————— 62
Swiss Mocha —————————— 63
Filipino Barako Coffee ——————— 64

Hawaiian Macadamia Nut Coffee ——— 65
Austrian Wiener Melange ————— 66
American Pumpkin Spice Latte ———— 67
Israeli Coffee Hafuch ——————— 68
Nigerian Coffee —————————— 69
Vietnamese Coffee ———————— 70
Egyptian Sada Coffee ——————— 71
Puerto Rican Café con Leche ———— 72
Indonesian Kopi Tubruk —————— 73
Indonesian Pandan Coffee ————— 74
Japanese Kyoto-style Cold Brew ——— 75
Belgian Speculoos Latte —————— 76
Brazilian Cinnamon Coffee ————— 78
Mexican Spicy Mocha ——————— 79
Lebanese Cardamom Coffee ———— 80
Chinese Red Bean Coffee —————— 81
Guatemalan Atol de Elote Coffee ——— 82
Peruvian Inca Mocha ——————— 84
Colombian Caramel Macchiato ——— 85
French Caramel Macchiato ————— 86
South Korean Banana Latte ———— 87
Japanese Espresso Tonic —————— 88
Dutch Koffie Verkeerd ——————— 89
Ecuadorian Quaker Coffee ————— 90
South African Gemmer Koffie ———— 91
Canadian Maple Latte ——————— 92

# Chapter 8: Iced Coffee Delights ———————————————————— 93

Brazilian Caipirinha Coffee ————— 94
Spanish Horchata Iced Coffee ———— 95
German Eiskaffee ————————— 96
Thai Coconut Iced Coffee —————— 97
Mexican Chocolate Iced Coffee ——— 98
Hawaiian Pineapple Iced Coffee ——— 99

Australian Iced Caramel Latte ———— 100
Australian Iced Mocha ——————— 101
Vietnamese Iced Coffee —————— 102
Thai Iced Coffee ————————— 103
British Iced Mocha ———————— 104
Thai Thai Iced Tea Coffee —————— 105

# BONUS: How to Accompany Coffee ———————————————————— 106

# Conclusion ———————————————————————————————— 108

# Introduction

In the realm of sensory pleasures, few experiences can rival the alluring embrace of a well-brewed cup of coffee. This humble bean, transformed by the alchemy of heat and water, has evolved into an art form that transcends borders, cultures, and centuries. It is a testament to the human capacity to refine and elevate the simplest of substances into a symphony of flavors, aromas, and sensations.

Coffee, the elixir of alert minds and weary souls, traces its roots deep into the annals of history, weaving a narrative as rich and complex as the beverage itself. Its journey is a testament to humanity's enduring quest for the extraordinary in the everyday, a story of transformation and innovation that has, over the ages, melded tradition with invention. In the following pages, we embark on a voyage through time to explore the historical origins of coffee, and delve into the captivating art of coffee as we know it today.

At its core, coffee is a symbol of transformation. Its story begins in the highlands of East Africa, where the coffee plant, scientifically known as Coffea, found its natural habitat. In those lush and mountainous regions, indigenous communities discovered the potential of coffee cherries, their vibrant red fruit concealing the precious seeds we now call coffee beans. The age-old practice of cultivating and roasting these beans was the inception of a journey that would eventually take coffee across continents and cultures.

As the coffee plant's seeds traversed the globe, the art of coffee began to take shape. With each new region and culture that embraced coffee, the brew underwent a metamorphosis, evolving into a reflection of local tastes, customs, and desires. Whether it was the elegant Turkish coffee rituals, the enchanting Italian espresso culture, or the laid-back American coffee shop scene, each incarnation carried the unique spirit of its creators. Coffee was not just a drink; it was a canvas for creativity and self-expression.

The art of coffee can be defined by its ability to encapsulate a multitude of senses. From the moment the beans are ground and the aroma escapes, to the sound of hot water cascading over the grounds and the first sip that awakens the taste buds, coffee is a multi-dimensional experience. Its taste profile is a symphony of bitter and sweet, acidity and body, with a range of flavors that span from earthy and nutty to fruity and floral. Every cup, every brew method, and every barista's touch yields a unique masterpiece.

Over the years, the art of coffee has undergone a remarkable transformation. From the traditional methods of boiling coffee over open fires to the modern marvels of espresso machines and pour-over devices, the tools and techniques have evolved in parallel with our understanding of the bean's complexity. Coffee shops have become cultural hubs, where the pursuit of the perfect cup is celebrated as both a science and an art. The journey of coffee is a reflection of our changing world, mirroring the technological and cultural shifts of our time.

In the following chapters, we will delve deeper into the intricacies of the art of coffee. We will explore the diverse coffee cultures around the world, the cultivation and processing of coffee beans, the various brewing methods, and the passionate individuals who have dedicated their lives to the pursuit of coffee perfection. Through this exploration, we aim to reveal the enchanting journey that has brought us to the coffee culture we cherish today.

Join us on this odyssey through time, as we uncover the captivating history and artistry of coffee, and savor the ever-evolving brew that has become an inseparable part of our lives. From its birthplace in Africa to the bustling coffeehouses of the modern world, coffee has thrived and transformed, reflecting our collective creativity, passion, and desire to experience the extraordinary in the ordinary.

Welcome to the world of coffee—an art as diverse and captivating as the human spirit itself.

# Chapter 1:
# The Great Variety of Coffee

In the vast and diverse landscape of coffee, one is faced with a world of choices. From the fertile highlands of Ethiopia to the lush terrains of Colombia and the volcanic soils of Java, coffee beans are cultivated in a remarkable array of locations, each with its own unique attributes. The coffee connoisseur's journey is one of exploration, guided by a desire to savor the full spectrum of flavors, aromas, and experiences that coffee has to offer. In this chapter, we embark on a sensory voyage to explore the great variety of coffee, where differences in flavor, origin, and fragrance create a tapestry of tastes that beguile and delight the discerning palate.

## The Many Types of Coffee

Coffee, the ubiquitous elixir that has captured the hearts of people around the world, is not just a single, uniform drink. It's a diverse and multifaceted beverage, with a vast array of styles, preparations, and variations that cater to every palate and preference. From the straightforward black coffee to the complex and artful espresso-based concoctions, the world of coffee is rich with choices that cater to diverse tastes and cultural traditions.

1. The Classics: Black Coffee

Let's begin with the basics. A cup of black coffee, unadulterated by milk, sugar, or flavorings, is a timeless classic. The simple and straightforward nature of black coffee allows the flavors of the beans to shine through. Whether it's a single-origin specialty brew or a reliable cup from your trusted local diner, black coffee is the foundation upon which the coffee world is built.

## 2. Espresso: The Heart of Italian Tradition

The tiny but mighty espresso shot has played an integral role in Italian coffee culture for generations. It's a concentrated coffee, brewed by forcing hot water through finely ground coffee beans. The result is a potent and intense flavor that's the basis for many other coffee drinks. Espresso is often served as a single shot, but it's also the foundation of various other coffee creations, such as cappuccinos, lattes, and Americanos.

## 3. Cappuccino: The Perfect Balance

A cappuccino is a harmonious blend of espresso, steamed milk, and milk foam. The ideal cappuccino strikes a perfect balance between the rich intensity of espresso and the creamy smoothness of milk, topped with a frothy foam cap. It's a beverage that's beloved for its elegance and depth of flavor.

## 4. Latte: Creamy and Comforting

If you prefer your coffee on the milder side, the latte might be your go-to choice. It's a mix of espresso and steamed milk, resulting in a smooth and creamy coffee with a gentle coffee flavor. Lattes are often favored by those who appreciate a comforting and mild coffee experience.

## 5. Americano: Espresso's Easygoing Cousin

An Americano is a simple yet effective way to dilute the intensity of espresso. It's made by adding hot water to a shot of espresso, resulting in a beverage with the strength of espresso but a milder flavor profile. Americanos are popular among those who enjoy a straightforward coffee flavor with a bit less punch.

## 6. Macchiato: Espresso with a Mark

A macchiato, which means "stained" or "spotted" in Italian, is a shot of espresso "stained" or "marked" with a small amount of frothy milk. It's a delicate balance between the boldness of espresso and the gentle touch of milk, creating a coffee that's both strong and nuanced.

## 7. Mocha: Coffee Meets Chocolate

For those with a sweet tooth, the mocha is the perfect indulgence. It combines espresso, steamed milk, and chocolate, resulting in a rich, decadent coffee drink. A well-prepared mocha is a delightful fusion of coffee and cocoa, offering a comforting and sweet experience.

## 8. Affogato: Coffee and Dessert in One

The affogato is a simple yet indulgent treat that combines a shot of hot espresso poured over a scoop of vanilla ice cream. The hot-cold, coffee-ice cream contrast is a delightful interplay of flavors and textures, making it a popular choice for a quick and satisfying dessert.

## 9. Turkish Coffee: A Taste of Tradition

Traveling eastward, Turkish coffee is a cherished part of Middle Eastern and Balkan traditions. It's made by finely grinding coffee beans and simmering them with water and sugar (if desired) in a special pot called a cezve or ibrik. The result is a rich, unfiltered coffee with a sludge of grounds at the bottom of the cup. Turkish coffee is often enjoyed with a side of sweet treats and carries a rich cultural significance.

## 10. Cold Brew: Coffee Chilled to Perfection

When the weather warms up, cold brew steps into the spotlight. This coffee style is made by steeping coarsely ground coffee beans in cold water for an extended period, often 12-24 hours. The result is a smooth, low-acid coffee that's served over ice. Cold brew has gained popularity for its refreshing and mild taste, making it a favorite for those seeking a caffeine kick without the bitterness.

## 11. Nitro Coffee: Coffee Takes a Tap

Nitro coffee is a relatively recent innovation that takes cold brew to the next level. It's cold brew coffee infused with nitrogen gas and served on tap, much like draft beer. The result is a creamy, effervescent coffee with a frothy head, similar to a stout beer. Nitro coffee's unique texture and taste have made it a hit in many coffee shops.

## 12. Single-Origin Coffees: A Taste of Place

For the discerning coffee enthusiast, single-origin coffees offer a fascinating journey into the world of terroir. These beans are sourced from a specific region or even a single estate, allowing you to explore the distinct flavors and aromas associated with that locale. Whether it's a Kenyan AA with bright acidity or a Sumatra Mandheling with earthy richness, single-origin coffees are a direct link to the coffee's place of origin.

The world of coffee is a treasure trove of choices, and this chapter only scratches the surface. Each coffee style represents a unique blend of tradition, innovation, and cultural influence, creating a wide spectrum of flavors and experiences to satisfy every coffee lover's palate. Whether you savor the classics or delight in exploring new coffee frontiers, the world of coffee is an ever-evolving adventure of taste and discovery.

## Differences in Flavor

Beyond the botanical and processing distinctions, the flavor of coffee is heavily influenced by its terroir, the unique combination of climate, soil, altitude, and geography in which the beans are grown. Each region imparts its own fingerprint on the beans, resulting in a remarkable range of flavors.

Let's start our journey in the birthplace of coffee, Ethiopia. Here, in the lush and mountainous regions, you'll find some of the world's most renowned coffee varieties. Ethiopian coffee is known for its intricate flavors, often carrying fruity, floral, and herbal notes. Yirgacheffe, Sidamo, and Harrar are just a few of the celebrated coffee regions in this cradle of coffee culture.

Moving south to Kenya, coffee takes on a bright and lively character. Kenyan coffee beans are celebrated for their vibrant acidity, often described as sharp and citric, with undertones of blackcurrant, tomato, and bright citrus. The Kenyan AA grade coffee is a classic example of the region's distinct flavor profile.

In contrast, the Central and South American coffee-producing countries, such as Colombia, Costa Rica, and Panama, offer coffee with a milder and more balanced profile. These regions are celebrated for their smooth, medium-bodied coffees with a bright acidity, making them popular choices for many coffee enthusiasts. Colombian coffee, in particular, is revered for its versatility and is often a staple in blends due to its consistent quality.

Further south, we encounter the high-altitude coffee regions of Peru and Bolivia, where coffee cherries are cultivated in pristine conditions. These beans often exhibit notes of dark chocolate, nuts, and a pronounced sweetness. The combination of altitude and rich volcanic soil lends these coffees a unique charm that captivates the senses.

If you prefer a coffee with a rich, earthy depth, consider exploring Indonesian varieties. The coffee from Sumatra, Java, and Sulawesi is famous for its full-bodied, spicy, and sometimes earthy flavors, making it an excellent choice for those who enjoy a more robust and complex cup.

In the Americas, the Hawaiian islands, particularly Kona, produce coffee that stands apart with its distinctive nutty and mildly fruity flavors. The volcanic soil and tropical climate create an environment uniquely suited to coffee cultivation.

On the African continent, the coffee from regions like Tanzania and Uganda also offers a diverse and intriguing range of flavors. These coffees are often characterized by their bright acidity and a mix of fruity, floral, and herbal notes.

Ethiopian Elegance: Coffee's birthplace, Ethiopia, offers a vibrant spectrum of flavors. Ethiopian coffee is known for its floral and fruity notes, often accompanied by a refreshing brightness. The Yirgacheffe region, for instance, is celebrated for its distinct lemony acidity and floral aroma, while Harrar coffee presents a full-bodied, earthy character with wine-like undertones.

Kenyan Acidity: Kenyan coffee is renowned for its bright and intense acidity, characterized by flavors that range from blackcurrant and tomato to bright citrus notes. These beans often carry a remarkable liveliness that sets them apart in the world of coffee.

South American Smoothness: Central and South American coffee-producing countries, such as Colombia, Costa Rica, and Brazil, offer coffee with a milder and more balanced profile. These beans are known for their smooth, medium-bodied character, often with bright acidity, making them popular choices for many coffee enthusiasts.

Exotic Indonesian Varieties: Indonesian coffees, like those from Sumatra and Java, offer a rich and earthy depth, often described as spicy and sometimes smoky. These beans are revered for their full body and complex, wild flavors.

African Diversity: African coffees, from countries like Tanzania and Uganda, offer a diverse and intriguing range of flavors. These beans are often characterized by bright acidity and a mix of fruity, floral, and herbal notes.

Hawaiian Richness: Hawaiian coffee, particularly Kona coffee from the Big Island, carries a distinctive nutty and mildly fruity profile. The volcanic soil and tropical climate create an environment uniquely suited to coffee cultivation.

The Charm of Bolivian and Peruvian Coffee: High-altitude coffee regions of Bolivia and Peru offer beans that often carry notes of dark chocolate, nuts, and a pronounced sweetness. These coffees thrive in pristine conditions that elevate their unique charm.

The combination of these terroirs contributes to a remarkable diversity of coffee flavors, ensuring that every region offers a new and intriguing taste adventure.

## The Allure of Fragrance

While taste and origin are essential components of the coffee experience, the fragrance or aroma of coffee is equally captivating. The fragrance can be a precursor to the delightful symphony of flavors that await in the brewed cup.

Arabica coffees often exhibit a wide range of fragrances, from floral and fruity to nutty and spicy. When you inhale the aroma of a freshly ground Arabica coffee, you may detect hints of jasmine, citrus blossoms, or berries. These delicate fragrances hint at the complex and nuanced flavors that lie within.

In contrast, Robusta beans have a more earthy and woody fragrance, often reminiscent of earth, cedar, or nuts. These scents mirror the robust and bitter profile of the beans when brewed.

The processing method also plays a significant role in a coffee's fragrance. Natural coffees, with their retained fruit pulp, often exude intense fruity and wine-like fragrances. Washed coffees, on the other hand, have a cleaner, crisper scent, often with bright floral and herbal notes.

In the world of coffee, the variations in fragrance are as diverse as the regions themselves. Ethiopian coffees might offer the enchanting aroma of jasmine and bergamot, while a Kenyan coffee can entice you with the scent of ripe berries. A Colombian coffee may evoke the fragrance of fresh-cut apples, while an Indonesian bean might release the rich, earthy aromas of the forest.

The complexity of coffee fragrance is a prelude to the sensory symphony that unfolds as you brew and savor your chosen beans. The interplay of fragrance, flavor, and origin is what makes coffee a fascinating and continually evolving art form.

The world of coffee is a canvas of diversity, where the subtlest differences in flavor, origin, and fragrance paint a vibrant tapestry of choices. From the highlands of Ethiopia to the volcanic slopes of Indonesia, from the bright acidity of Kenyan coffee to the mellow richness of Colombian beans, the options are as varied as the cultures that nurture them. Whether you seek a floral and fruity adventure or a bold and earthy experience, coffee offers a multitude of paths to explore and enjoy.

In the chapters that follow, we will delve deeper into these unique coffee regions and their respective offerings. We will explore the cultivation, processing, and brewing techniques that allow each bean to shine in its own right. Coffee's variety is a testament to the power of nature, the craft of farming, and the artistry of roasting and brewing. It is a world waiting to be explored, one cup at a time.

1. The Aromatic Prelude

The journey of coffee aroma begins when the beans are freshly ground. Coffee connoisseurs are well-acquainted with the intoxicating scent that wafts through the air as the grinder does its work. This initial burst of fragrance is the first hint of the flavors that will soon grace your palate.

The aroma of freshly ground coffee can be a tantalizing mix of earthy, nutty, floral, and fruity notes. It is a sensory overture that sets the stage for the brew to come.

2. The Delicate Bouquet of Coffee Flowers

Before coffee cherries transform into beans, they undergo a fleeting phase where they blossom into fragrant coffee flowers. This moment of bloom, although short-lived, contributes to the overall aroma and flavor profile of the beans.

Coffee flowers release a delicate, slightly sweet scent that can be compared to jasmine or citrus blossoms. While the flowers' aroma doesn't directly translate to the coffee's flavor, it's a reminder of the intricate processes that give birth to the beans.

3. The Richness of Roasted Beans

Roasting, the alchemical process that turns green coffee beans into the aromatic brew we love, is the apex of coffee fragrance. When coffee beans are roasted, a myriad of volatile compounds that make up their complex aroma is released.

Roasters carefully orchestrate the roasting process to accentuate the specific flavor compounds that will contribute to the coffee's unique fragrance. The aromas that emerge are a kaleidoscope of notes, from fruity and floral to spicy and smoky, all encapsulated in the humble coffee bean.

4. The Impact of Processing Method

The coffee bean's fragrance is also influenced by the processing method. For instance, natural or dry-processed coffees, where the cherries are dried with the fruit intact, often exhibit intense fruity and wine-like fragrances. This comes from the prolonged contact between the beans and the cherries.

On the other hand, washed coffees, where the cherries are depulped and fermented before drying, result in a cleaner and crisper scent, often with bright floral and herbal notes.

## 5. The First Whiff of Brewed Coffee

The most anticipated moment in the coffee journey is that first whiff of freshly brewed coffee. The aroma that wafts from the cup is a revelation of the coffee's potential. It carries the promise of the flavors that will soon caress your taste buds.

The brewed coffee aroma can range from earthy and nutty to fruity and floral, depending on the origin and roast of the beans. It is an enchanting prelude to the symphony of flavors that unfold with each sip.

## 6. The Pleasure of Aroma in Coffee Tasting

Coffee cupping, the professional practice of evaluating coffee, places a strong emphasis on aroma. Before tasting the coffee, participants take in the fragrance by deeply inhaling the aroma from the freshly brewed coffee grounds. This step, often referred to as "breaking the crust," provides insights into the coffee's overall character and quality.

The fragrance of coffee can be a remarkable experience, as it evolves and reveals different facets with each passing moment. The heady initial burst gives way to subtler, more nuanced notes, allowing tasters to uncover the intricate layers of aroma within the coffee.

## 7. The Aromas of the World

Coffee's aromas, much like its flavors, are influenced by the bean's geographical origin. Ethiopian coffees might offer the enchanting aroma of jasmine and bergamot, while a Kenyan coffee can entice you with the scent of ripe berries. A Colombian coffee may evoke the fragrance of fresh-cut apples, while an Indonesian bean might release the rich, earthy aromas of the forest.

The aroma of coffee is a reminder of the world's diverse terroirs, each contributing to the rich tapestry of coffee fragrances that captivate and enthrall coffee enthusiasts around the globe.

## 8. The Scent of Memory

Coffee aroma has a unique power to evoke memories and emotions. The smell of a particular coffee blend may transport you to a cozy café in Paris, a bustling street market in Marrakech, or a quiet morning in your childhood home.

For many, the aroma of coffee is a deeply personal and nostalgic experience, connecting them to cherished moments and places. It is a fragrance that transcends the mere act of drinking coffee, serving as a bridge to the past and a portal to cherished memories. In the world of coffee, fragrance is not merely a sensory pleasure; it is a symphony that invites you to explore the depths of culture, geography, and memory. The allure of coffee aroma is a timeless and enchanting part of the coffee experience, one that enriches the journey from the moment the beans are ground to the last lingering scent in your cup.

# Chapter 2:
# From Harvesting to Roasting

In the world of coffee, the journey from bean to brew is a complex and fascinating process, where countless variables come together to shape the flavor, aroma, and character of the final cup. From the moment coffee cherries are plucked from the tree to the precise temperatures of the roasting drum, every step in this journey is critical to unlocking the full potential of the coffee bean. In this chapter, we will embark on a journey through the stages of coffee production, from harvesting to roasting, exploring the techniques and practices that transform a humble cherry into a captivating brew.

## Harvesting Coffee Cherries

The journey of coffee begins with the delicate process of harvesting the coffee cherries. While coffee cherries appear uniform at a distance, their ripeness can vary greatly, and the timing of the harvest is crucial to the quality of the beans. In coffee-producing regions around the world, the harvest typically falls into one of two categories: selective picking or strip picking.

Selective Picking: This method involves harvesting only the ripest cherries. Skilled laborers navigate the coffee fields, carefully selecting the cherries at their peak of ripeness and leaving unripe or overripe ones on the branch. Selective picking ensures that the beans are of the highest quality and are ready for processing. It is a labor-intensive process, as it requires multiple passes through the same tree over the course of the harvest season.

Strip Picking: In contrast, strip picking involves harvesting all the cherries on a branch, regardless of their ripeness. This method is often quicker and more efficient but can result in a mixture of ripe and unripe beans. Strip picking is commonly used for less expensive coffees or in regions with a shorter harvest window.

Once the cherries are collected, they are transported to a processing facility, where the next crucial steps in coffee production unfold.

1. The Perfect Timing

Coffee cherries are the vibrant, cherry-like fruits that encase the coffee beans. The timing of their harvest is a delicate dance. It's a crucial decision for coffee farmers as it profoundly influences the flavor and quality of the beans.

The key to a successful coffee harvest lies in selecting cherries at the peak of ripeness. The color of the cherries is a reliable indicator of their readiness. They transition from green to a vibrant red or yellow hue, depending on the coffee variety. The selection of only the ripest cherries ensures the optimal sweetness and flavor of the beans.

2. Handpicking: A Labor of Love

In many coffee-growing regions, the cherries are meticulously handpicked by skilled workers. Handpicking allows for selective harvesting, ensuring that only the ripe cherries are chosen. This labor-intensive method is not only a tradition but also an art, as pickers deftly pluck the cherries without damaging the delicate branches.

Skilled coffee pickers are highly valued in the industry, as their expertise in selecting the right cherries is essential for producing high-quality coffee. They navigate the dense foliage, expertly identifying and plucking the cherries at the perfect moment. Handpicking requires both precision and a deep connection to the coffee plants.

3. The Stripping Method

In some regions, particularly where coffee cultivation is on a larger scale, the "stripping" method is employed. This technique involves collecting the entire branch of cherries in one go. While it's less selective than handpicking, it is often a more efficient method for larger coffee operations.

In the stripping method, all the cherries, regardless of their ripeness, are harvested together. Afterward, the cherries are sorted to separate the ripe from the unripe. This method can lead to higher yields but may come at the cost of bean quality, as the unripe cherries can affect the flavor of the final coffee.

4. Mechanical Harvesting

In some modern coffee farms, particularly those with flat terrain and large acreages, mechanical harvesters are employed. These machines are designed to shake the coffee plants, causing the cherries to fall onto a conveyor belt. Mechanical harvesting is efficient and can handle large quantities quickly, but it is less selective than handpicking, and the cherries collected may include some unripe ones.

Mechanical harvesting is more common in regions where the focus is on producing large quantities of coffee, often for commercial purposes. It can be a pragmatic approach in such cases, as it significantly reduces labor costs and accelerates the harvest process.

## Processing Coffee Beans

The journey of coffee cherries doesn't end with their careful harvest; it continues with the processing of coffee beans. This crucial step in the coffee production cycle involves transforming the cherries into the green coffee beans that are ready for roasting and, eventually, brewing. The processing method chosen significantly influences the flavor, aroma, and quality of the final coffee product.

1. The Three Primary Processing Methods

There are three primary methods for processing coffee beans: dry or natural processing, wet or washed processing, and honey processing. Each method imparts distinct characteristics to the beans and contributes to the final flavor profile.

a. Dry or Natural Processing

In the dry or natural processing method, the whole coffee cherries, including the fruit, are spread out to dry in the sun. This process can take several weeks, during which the cherries are turned periodically to ensure uniform drying. Once fully dried, the cherries are mechanically or manually hulled to reveal the beans inside.

Natural processed coffees often have a robust, fruity flavor profile with wine-like undertones. The extended contact with the cherry's pulp during drying imparts unique fruity and floral notes to the beans, making them a favorite for those who appreciate bold and complex flavors.

b. Wet or Washed Processing

Wet or washed processing is a method that involves depulping the cherries immediately after harvest. The beans are then soaked in water for fermentation, which helps to remove the sticky mucilage layer that surrounds the beans. The beans are then thoroughly washed and dried, often on raised beds or patios.

Washed coffees tend to have a cleaner, crisper taste, with brighter acidity and distinct flavors. The removal of the mucilage at an early stage in the process allows the beans to develop a more focused and well-defined flavor profile. This method is favored by those who enjoy a balanced and refined coffee experience.

c. Honey-Processed Coffee

Honey processing is a method that strikes a balance between the natural and washed methods. In this process, the cherries are partially depulped, leaving some of the fruit intact, and then dried. This partial depulping results in a sweet, sticky layer, often referred to as "honey," that clings to the beans.

Honey-processed coffees carry a unique sweetness and complexity, as the residual honey-like layer contributes to their flavor. The beans can range from "white honey" with minimal mucilage to "red honey" with more fruit residue, each offering distinct flavor profiles.

2. The Role of Processing in Flavor Development

The choice of processing method significantly impacts the final flavor profile of the coffee. The method used can enhance or diminish certain flavor characteristics, influencing the overall taste and aroma.

For instance, natural processed coffees are often known for their bold and fruity notes, while washed coffees are celebrated for their clarity and distinct acidity. Honey-processed coffees, with their balance of sweetness and complexity, offer a unique flavor experience that falls between the other two methods.

3. Geographical Influences

The choice of processing method can also be influenced by the geographical location of the coffee farm. In some regions, environmental factors and climate conditions may favor one method over others.

For example, natural processing is often favored in areas with a dry climate, as it relies on sun drying. Washed processing, on the other hand, is more common in regions with access to abundant water resources.

4. Experimentation and Innovation

In recent years, the coffee industry has witnessed a surge in experimentation and innovation in processing methods. Coffee producers, especially in the realm of specialty coffee, are exploring new and creative techniques to enhance flavor profiles and create unique coffee experiences.

Methods such as anaerobic fermentation, carbonic maceration, and extended fermentation periods are gaining popularity. These methods push the boundaries of traditional processing to unlock new dimensions of flavor and aroma in coffee.

Processing coffee beans is a vital stage in the coffee production process, where the cherries' flavors and characteristics are shaped and refined. Whether it's the bold and fruity notes of natural processed coffees, the crisp clarity of washed coffees, or the balanced sweetness of honey-processed coffees, each method offers a distinct and captivating coffee experience. The processing journey is an art that brings forth the full potential of the coffee cherries, paving the way for the roasting stage and the creation of the coffee we savor and enjoy.

## Roasting Coffee Beans

Roasting is the transformative alchemy that turns green coffee beans into the aromatic and flavorful coffee we adore. It's a pivotal stage in the coffee production process, where a blend of art and science comes together to unlock the beans' full potential. The roasting process involves the careful application of heat and time to create the delightful flavors, aromas, and colors that define our favorite coffee brews.

1. The Green Bean Metamorphosis

Green coffee beans, straight from the fields, are dense, hard, and green in color. They lack the aromatic compounds and flavors that we associate with our daily cup of coffee. The roasting process is where the magical transformation occurs.

The beans are loaded into a roasting machine, which could be a traditional drum roaster or a more modern fluid-bed roaster. The machine's job is to subject the beans to carefully controlled heat.

2. The Roasting Stages

Roasting coffee beans typically consists of three main stages: drying, browning, and development. Each stage plays a crucial role in shaping the beans' flavors and aromas.

   a. Drying (Stage 1): This is the initial stage of roasting. The green coffee beans are introduced to heat, and their moisture content begins to evaporate. The temperature is gradually raised, reaching around 200 degrees Celsius. The beans expand and lose moisture, developing a yellowish tint.
   b. Browning (Stage 2): In the browning stage, which follows drying, the beans undergo a process called the Maillard reaction. This reaction is responsible for the browning of the beans and the development of flavor compounds. Sugars and amino acids react, creating the aromatic and flavorful compounds that characterize the taste of coffee. As the temperature rises, the beans change from yellow to light brown and then to a deeper shade, releasing a heady aroma.
   c. Development (Stage 3): The final stage, development, is where the beans reach their desired roast level. The roaster closely monitors the beans, adjusting the temperature and duration to achieve the perfect balance of acidity, body, and flavor. This phase is critical, as it requires precision to bring out the beans' unique qualities.

3. Roasting Profiles

Roasting profiles are specific heat and time settings used to achieve desired flavor and aroma characteristics. Roasters create profiles that align with the coffee's origin, variety, and the final taste they wish to achieve. For instance, a light roast profile might preserve the coffee's bright acidity, while a darker roast can emphasize a full body and bold flavor.

## 4. The Role of the Roaster

Roasting coffee is both an art and a science, and the roaster plays a pivotal role in the process. It's up to the roaster to select the right beans, choose the optimal roast profile, and skillfully control the roasting machine to produce the desired flavor and aroma.

Professional coffee roasters often rely on their senses, experience, and technical expertise to create the perfect roast. They use their eyes, ears, and noses to monitor the beans, adjusting the heat and airflow as needed. Roasters may also employ computerized systems to maintain precise control over temperature and timing.

## 5. The Color and Complexity of Roasts

The length of time the beans spend in the roaster, the peak temperature, and the cooling process after roasting all contribute to the beans' color and complexity. Light roasts are generally lighter in color and retain the most of the beans' original characteristics. As the roast deepens, the beans become darker, and the flavor profile shifts, with the beans losing some of their origin-specific qualities in favor of roast-driven notes.

## 6. Cooling and Resting

After the beans have reached their desired roast level, they need to be quickly cooled to stop the roasting process. This is typically achieved with a flow of cool air. Once cooled, the beans are often allowed to rest for a period ranging from a few hours to a few days. This resting phase, known as "degassing," allows the beans to release carbon dioxide accumulated during roasting and stabilize their flavors.

Roasting coffee beans is an art that requires a deep understanding of the beans' characteristics, precise control over the roasting process, and a keen sensory perception. The roaster's skill and expertise are instrumental in crafting the flavor and aroma of the final cup of coffee. Roasting is where the green beans' potential is fully realized, creating the aromatic and flavorful experience that coffee enthusiasts eagerly anticipate with every brew.

# Chapter 3:
# It's Not Just About Coffee

Coffee is more than just a beverage; it's a sensory journey. Beyond the coffee's origin, roast level, and brewing method, several factors come into play to affect the taste and aroma of your cup. In this chapter, we'll explore these crucial elements and delve into the art of selecting the perfect coffee beans to match your preferences.

## Moisture Content and Temperature

In the realm of coffee, the moisture content and temperature are foundational factors that profoundly influence the beans' flavor, aroma, and overall quality. Understanding and managing these elements are crucial in the journey from green coffee beans to the perfect roast.

The Crucial Balance

Green coffee beans arrive with a natural moisture content, typically ranging between 9% and 12%. This moisture level is vital for a consistent and controlled roasting process. Beans with insufficient moisture may roast unevenly, leading to a lack of complexity and flat flavors. On the contrary, beans with excessive moisture may roast inconsistently, resulting in an unsatisfactory taste.

Roasters meticulously monitor and manage the moisture content. It's a delicate balance to ensure that the beans reach their optimal state for roasting. Too little moisture can result in rapid roasting and loss of flavor nuances, while excess moisture can impede even roasting.

Impact of Temperature: Crafting the Flavor Profile

Temperature during roasting is the linchpin for crafting the beans' flavor profile. The rate of temperature rise, the peak temperature reached, and the cooling process significantly influence the beans' taste and aroma.

The journey from the initial drying phase to the final development stage is a symphony of temperature and time. It's here that the beans transition from their initial green hue to various shades of brown, with the Maillard reaction unlocking a tapestry of flavors. The beans' temperature progression during roasting is the key to capturing the desired characteristics—whether it's bright acidity, caramelized sweetness, or rich, chocolatey depth.

Precision in Roasting

Roasting coffee beans is a precision art. Roasters carefully control the rate of temperature increase, the duration of each stage, and the final cooling to curate the perfect roast. This artistry demands keen observation, experience, and understanding of how moisture and temperature interplay to develop the desired flavors.

The roasted beans' aroma, color, and taste are a testament to the roaster's ability to orchestrate the moisture content and temperature precisely. It's this marriage of science and sensory finesse that yields the diverse and enticing flavors found in each cup of coffee.

The Balanced Blend

The roasting process isn't solely about achieving a particular color or a set temperature; it's about balancing these elements to bring out the beans' finest characteristics. The moisture content and temperature management, when precisely coordinated, produce a symphony of flavors unique to each batch of coffee.

Ultimately, the magic of roasting lies in how roasters harness moisture content and temperature, teasing out the nuances in the beans and transforming them into the flavorful brews that delight coffee enthusiasts worldwide.

## Deciphering Coffee Labels

When selecting coffee beans, the label on the bag offers valuable insights into the coffee's characteristics. Here's how to decode the information and choose the right coffee for your taste preferences:

   a. Origin: The coffee's place of origin is a fundamental factor in its flavor profile. Coffee labels typically include information about the country or region where the beans were grown. For example, a Colombian coffee may have a balanced and nutty flavor, while an Ethiopian coffee might be bright and floral.
   b. Varietals: Coffee varietals refer to the specific subspecies or cultivar of the coffee plant. Different varietals can produce a wide range of flavors. For example, Geisha coffee is

known for its vibrant floral and fruity notes, while Bourbon beans are celebrated for their sweetness and complexity.
c. Processing Method: The processing method, as discussed in the previous chapter, can significantly influence flavor. Whether the coffee is natural, washed, honey-processed, or subject to other innovative methods, this information will be on the label.
d. Roast Level: The roast level is a key factor in determining the flavor profile of your coffee. Coffee labels often indicate whether the beans are light, medium, or dark roasted. Light roasts tend to preserve the beans' origin-specific qualities, while dark roasts develop deeper, roast-driven flavors.
e. Tasting Notes: Many coffee labels include tasting notes, which describe the coffee's flavor and aroma characteristics. These notes may range from fruity and floral to nutty and chocolatey. Pay attention to these descriptions to get a sense of what to expect from the coffee.
f. Intensity: Some coffee brands use a scale to indicate the coffee's intensity. This scale can help you understand whether the coffee is mellow and mild or bold and robust. It's a useful guide for selecting coffee that matches your taste preferences.

## Personal Preferences and Experimentation

In the world of coffee, your personal preferences play a significant role in shaping your coffee journey. Coffee is more than a one-size-fits-all experience; it's a realm of flavors and aromas waiting to be explored, tailored to your unique taste. Here, we'll explore the importance of personal preferences and the joy of experimentation in your coffee adventure.

Evolving Tastes

Your taste in coffee, much like your taste in music or art, can evolve over time. What you enjoyed as your first cup of coffee may not align with your current preferences. This evolution is a natural part of your coffee journey.

As you delve deeper into the world of coffee, you may discover new flavors, aromas, and brew methods that resonate with your palate. What you love today may differ from what you crave tomorrow. Embrace the fluidity of your coffee taste and be open to trying new coffee experiences.

Exploration and Discovery

Coffee offers an endless array of flavor profiles, thanks to its diverse origins, varietals, processing methods, and roast levels. Your coffee journey is a quest for the perfect cup that aligns with your preferences.

Don't hesitate to explore different coffee beans, brewing techniques, and flavor notes. Whether it's a single-origin Ethiopian coffee with its bright acidity and floral aroma or a well-balanced blend, the world of coffee offers a treasure trove of options to suit every palate.

Boldness and Balance

Coffee comes in various profiles, from mellow and mild to bold and robust. The degree of boldness is often expressed on the coffee label using an intensity rating. By understanding your preferred level of boldness, you can select coffee that matches your taste.

If you enjoy a mild and delicate coffee, you might gravitate toward light roasts and low-intensity beans. For those who savor the rich, full-bodied experience, dark roasts and high-intensity coffee may be the choice. Your coffee journey is about finding the perfect balance between boldness and nuance.

Personalized Brewing

Brewing coffee is an art in itself. The grind size, water temperature, brew time, and the equipment you use can all affect the final taste and aroma of your coffee. Personalizing your brewing method is a way to craft your ideal cup.

Experiment with different brewing techniques to see how they influence the flavors and aromas of your coffee. Whether it's pour-over, French press, AeroPress, or espresso, each method offers a unique coffee experience. Your personalized brewing approach can elevate your coffee ritual to new heights.

The Joy of Experimentation

One of the most exciting aspects of the coffee journey is the opportunity to experiment and innovate. Coffee is not just about consumption; it's about creation and exploration. Home baristas and coffee enthusiasts worldwide are continually pushing the boundaries of coffee by trying new techniques, blending beans, and even roasting their own coffee.

Experimentation can lead to delightful discoveries. By trying different beans, roast levels, and brewing methods, you can unlock a world of flavors and aromas that cater to your preferences. Your coffee journey becomes a canvas for your creativity and a playground for your taste buds.

## The Art of Brewing

Brewing coffee is a craft that allows you to transform those carefully selected beans into a delicious and aromatic cup of your favorite beverage. It's where science and art intersect, and the outcome depends on your skills, equipment, and understanding of the brewing process. In this subchapter, we'll explore the key elements of the art of brewing coffee.

Quality Ingredients: The Foundation

Like any culinary masterpiece, the art of brewing coffee begins with quality ingredients. The main components are freshly roasted coffee beans and pure water. The quality of these ingredients will significantly impact the final brew.

a. Coffee Beans: Start with freshly roasted, high-quality coffee beans. Beans that are ground just before brewing provide the freshest flavor. The roast level and bean variety will also influence the taste.
b. Water: Water makes up the majority of your coffee, so its quality is paramount. Use clean, filtered water without impurities or strong odors. The ideal water temperature is around 200°F (93°C) to extract the flavors properly.

Grind Size: The Right Texture

The grind size of your coffee beans is a crucial factor. Different brewing methods require specific grind sizes to optimize flavor extraction.

a. Coarse Grind: French press brewing typically requires a coarse grind to prevent over-extraction.
b. Medium Grind: Drip coffee makers, pour-over methods, and AeroPress generally work well with a medium grind.
c. Fine Grind: Espresso machines need a fine grind for a short brew time and concentrated flavor.

Brewing Time: Finding the Sweet Spot

The brewing time is another variable to consider. It's the duration the water is in contact with the coffee grounds and has a direct impact on flavor. The ideal brewing time depends on your brewing method and the grind size.

a. Espresso: This method has a very short brewing time, usually around 25-30 seconds.
b. Drip Coffee: Drip coffee makers often take 5-7 minutes to complete the brewing process.
c. French Press: French press brewing usually lasts around 4 minutes.

Brew Ratios: Balance of Ingredients

The ratio of coffee to water is essential for achieving the desired strength. A general guideline is 1 to 2 tablespoons of coffee per 6 ounces of water, but you can adjust this to match your taste preferences.

# Chapter 4:
# Equipment Tips

The world of coffee is rich with various tools and machines that cater to different brewing methods, each offering its unique advantages and characteristics. In this chapter, we will explore a selection of coffee-making equipment, such as espresso machines, pour-over devices like the Melitta, Chemex, Hario V60, and Kalita Wave, along with the French press, Aeropress, and Siphon, and provide tips on how to get the best results from each.

## Espresso (Moka) Machine

The espresso machine, often referred to as a Moka pot, is a beloved and iconic stovetop coffee maker. This humble yet effective device has been a fixture in many coffee-loving households for generations. In this subchapter, we will explore the characteristics of the espresso machine and provide tips on how to make the most of it.

Description

The Moka pot consists of three chambers: a bottom chamber for water, a middle filter basket for coffee grounds, and an upper chamber to collect the brewed coffee. It operates on the principle of steam pressure, allowing water to pass through the coffee grounds and into the upper chamber.

Tips for Brewing with an Espresso (Moka) Machine

Choose the Right Grind: For a Moka pot, it's best to use finely ground coffee, similar to table salt. The fine grind allows for a balanced extraction and prevents water from passing through too quickly.

Fill the Filter Basket Evenly: Add coffee grounds to the filter basket but avoid packing them too tightly. A level and evenly distributed coffee bed will lead to a more consistent extraction.

Moderate Heat: Brew your coffee at a consistent, medium heat. This helps in preventing the coffee from scorching, which can lead to a bitter taste. It's crucial to find the right balance between heat and extraction time.

Keep an Eye on the Process: The Moka pot allows you to observe the brewing process directly. To avoid over-extraction, keep the lid open and pay attention to the coffee as it emerges in the upper chamber. Once the coffee starts to sputter, it's a sign that brewing is complete.

Use Fresh, Cold Water: Always use fresh, cold water when filling the bottom chamber. Using preheated water can lead to uneven extraction and less desirable flavors.

Clean Regularly: To maintain the quality of your Moka pot coffee, make sure to clean the device thoroughly after each use. Disassemble it, rinse all parts with warm water, and let them air dry. Avoid using soap or harsh detergents, as they can leave residue and affect the coffee's taste.

Experiment with Ratios: The strength of your Moka pot coffee can be adjusted by varying the coffee-to-water ratio. You can experiment with different ratios until you find the one that suits your taste preferences best.

Preheat the Moka Pot: Preheating the Moka pot by rinsing it with hot water before brewing can help maintain a consistent brewing temperature.

The Moka pot is a timeless and versatile coffee maker that allows you to create a bold, flavorful coffee in the comfort of your home. It offers a unique coffee experience that lies at the intersection of tradition and innovation, making it a beloved choice for many coffee enthusiasts. By understanding its characteristics and following these tips, you can consistently brew rich and aromatic coffee with your espresso (Moka) machine.

## Pour-Over Devices: Melitta, Chemex, Hario V60, Kalita Wave

Pour-over devices have gained popularity among coffee aficionados due to their ability to create clean and nuanced coffee. Each pour-over method offers its unique advantages, and in this subchapter, we will explore four popular pour-over devices: the Melitta, Chemex, Hario V60, and Kalita Wave.

## Melitta

The Melitta pour-over device is known for its simplicity and reliability. It consists of a cone-shaped plastic or ceramic dripper that sits on top of a coffee mug or carafe. Melitta paper filters are widely available and are an integral part of the brewing process.

Brewing Tips:

Use a medium grind coffee.

Pre-wet the paper filter with hot water to eliminate any paper taste.

Pour water in a circular motion to ensure even saturation of the coffee grounds.

Maintain a steady pour rate and water temperature to control extraction.

## Chemex

The Chemex is renowned for its elegant hourglass shape. It uses thick, bonded paper filters that produce a clean and crisp cup of coffee. The design is not only functional but also visually pleasing.

Brewing Tips:

Use a medium-coarse grind coffee, coarser than for most pour-over devices.

Pre-wet the filter and discard the rinse water.

Pour in a continuous spiral motion, starting from the center and moving outward.

Control the pour rate to achieve the desired strength and clarity.

## Hario V60

The Hario V60 is recognized for its conical shape and spiral ribs inside the dripper, which promotes an even extraction. It is available in various materials, including ceramic, glass, and plastic, making it a versatile choice.

Brewing Tips:

Opt for a medium grind coffee.

Pre-wet the filter to remove any papery taste and warm the dripper.

Pour water in spirals, moving from the center to the edges and back to the center.

Experiment with different pouring techniques to control the flow and extraction.

## Kalita Wave

The Kalita Wave is known for its flat-bottomed dripper and distinct wave filters. This design encourages an even extraction and a balanced cup of coffee. It's a favorite among those who appreciate a consistent brew.

Brewing Tips:

Use a medium to medium-coarse grind coffee.

Pre-wet the filter and let the water drain before adding coffee grounds.

Pour in a slow, controlled manner, making concentric circles.

Play with water temperature and pouring style to fine-tune the brew.

Each of these pour-over devices offers a unique brewing experience, allowing you to experiment with grind size, water temperature, pouring techniques, and more. They provide a platform for coffee enthusiasts to discover the nuances of flavor and aroma in their coffee. By understanding the specific characteristics of these devices and following the brewing tips, you can elevate your pour-over coffee game and create a cup that matches your taste preferences.

## French Press

The French press, also known as a press pot or plunger pot, is a timeless and beloved coffee brewing method. With its straightforward design and the ability to create a full-bodied, flavorful coffee, it has secured a special place in coffee culture. In this subchapter, we will delve into the characteristics of the French press and provide tips on how to make the most of it.

A French press consists of a cylindrical glass or stainless steel container and a plunger with a metal or mesh filter. The process is simple: coffee grounds are steeped in hot water, and after a few minutes, the plunger is pressed down to separate the coffee grounds from the liquid.

Brewing Tips:

Select the Right Grind: For the French press, it's advisable to use a coarse grind. This prevents fine coffee grounds from slipping through the filter, leading to a sediment-free cup.

Brew with Just-Off-the-Boil Water: Use water that's recently boiled but has had a minute or two to cool off slightly. The ideal water temperature is around 200°F (93°C).

Steep for the Appropriate Time: Let the coffee steep for about 4 minutes. You can adjust the steeping time slightly to suit your taste, but be cautious not to over-brew, which can result in bitterness.

Press Slowly and Evenly: When pressing down the plunger, do it slowly and evenly to avoid splashing or pushing grounds through the filter.

Decant Promptly: After brewing, it's essential to pour out the coffee immediately. Leaving the coffee in the French press can lead to over-extraction and a change in flavor.

Experiment with Ratios: The strength of your French press coffee can be adjusted by varying the coffee-to-water ratio. A general guideline is 1 to 2 tablespoons of coffee per 6 ounces of water, but you can fine-tune this to match your taste.

Maintenance and Cleaning: After each use, disassemble the French press and rinse all parts with warm water. Make sure to wash away all coffee residue, as it can affect the taste of future brews. Some French press models are dishwasher safe, but be sure to check the manufacturer's instructions.

The French press offers a direct and unadulterated way to experience coffee's full flavor and body. It's an excellent choice for those who appreciate a rich and robust cup of coffee. By following these brewing tips and understanding the nuances of the French press, you can consistently create a brew that matches your preferences.

## Aeropress

The Aeropress is a versatile and compact coffee maker known for its ability to produce a clean and flavorful cup of coffee. Developed by Alan Adler, the inventor of the Aerobie Frisbee, this brewing method has gained a dedicated following for its portability and flexibility. In this subchapter, we'll explore the characteristics of the Aeropress and provide tips on how to make the most of it.

The Aeropress is made up of a few simple components: a plastic brewing chamber, a plunger, and a filter cap. It operates on the principle of both immersion and pressure brewing. Coffee grounds are steeped in hot water, and the plunger is used to create pressure, forcing the coffee through a paper or metal filter.

Brewing Tips:

Choose the Right Grind: The Aeropress is versatile when it comes to grind size. You can experiment with different grinds, but a medium to fine grind often works well. The exact grind size can be adjusted to match your taste preferences.

Control the Water Temperature: Brew with water around 175-185°F (80-85°C). Using water that's too hot can lead to over-extraction and bitterness.

Play with Brewing Methods: The Aeropress offers the flexibility to experiment with different brewing methods. The standard method involves placing the Aeropress on a stable surface, while the inverted method starts with the Aeropress upside down.

Tinker with Brew Time: The steeping time can be adjusted to control the coffee's strength and flavor. The standard steeping time is around 30 seconds, but you can extend it slightly for a stronger brew.

Use the Plunger Gently: When using the plunger, apply gentle pressure. Forcing it down too quickly can cause splashing and may lead to over-extraction. A steady and gradual plunge is recommended.

Experiment with Ratios: The coffee-to-water ratio is adjustable. A general guideline is 1 to 2 tablespoons of coffee for every 6 ounces of water, but you can vary this to match your desired strength.

Consider the Inverted Method: The inverted method can be a game-changer for some Aeropress enthusiasts. It allows for longer steeping times and offers more control over the brewing process.

Cleaning and Maintenance: The Aeropress is easy to clean. After each use, disassemble it, remove the filter cap, and rinse all parts with warm water. The plunger seal should be occasionally lubricated with a bit of food-safe grease.

The Aeropress is an excellent choice for those who seek a portable, versatile, and consistent brewing method. It's perfect for coffee lovers on the go and those who enjoy experimenting with different parameters to fine-tune their coffee. By following these tips and embracing the flexibility of the Aeropress, you can consistently create a cup of coffee that aligns with your taste preferences.

## Siphon (Vacuum Pot)

The siphon, also known as a vacuum coffee maker or vacuum pot, is a fascinating and visually captivating method of brewing coffee. Its distinctive design and unique brewing process have made it a favorite among coffee aficionados who appreciate precision and flavor clarity. In this subchapter, we will explore the characteristics of the siphon and provide tips on how to make the most of this intriguing coffee-making device.

The siphon brewer consists of two chambers, typically made of glass or borosilicate, and connected by a tube. The lower chamber is filled with water, and the upper chamber holds the coffee grounds. A heat source, often an alcohol or butane burner, is used to create vapor pressure in the lower chamber, pushing the water into the upper chamber. Once brewing is complete, the heat source is removed, and the brewed coffee is drawn back down through a filter into the lower chamber.

Brewing Tips:

Choose the Right Grind: For the siphon, it's best to use a medium grind, similar to kosher salt. This grind size allows for an even extraction.

Experiment with Brew Time: The siphon brewing process is adjustable, allowing you to fine-tune the brew time. The optimal duration is typically 1 to 2 minutes.

Maintain a Consistent Water Temperature: It's crucial to keep the water temperature steady during the brewing process. A gooseneck kettle can be handy for precise water control.

Pre-Wet the Coffee Grounds: Before starting the brewing process, pre-wet the coffee grounds to ensure even saturation. This helps release the coffee's flavors more efficiently.

Handle with Care: The siphon's glass components can be delicate. When assembling and disassembling the brewer, handle it gently to avoid chipping or cracking.

Experiment with Ratios: The strength of your siphon coffee can be adjusted by varying the coffee-to-water ratio. You can experiment to find the ratio that matches your preferred strength.

Regular Cleaning and Maintenance: After each use, disassemble the siphon, remove the filter, and rinse all parts with warm water. Make sure to clean away any coffee residue that could affect the taste of future brews. Some siphon brewers are dishwasher safe, but refer to the manufacturer's instructions for maintenance.

The siphon (vacuum pot) offers a unique coffee experience that blends science and artistry. Its elaborate design and brewing process allow you to create a clean and precise cup of coffee that highlights the flavors and aromas of your chosen beans. By following these tips and understanding the intricacies of the siphon, you can consistently craft a cup of coffee that aligns with your taste preferences, all while enjoying the mesmerizing visual display of the brewing process.

# Chapter 5:
# Perfecting Your Coffee Brewing Skills

Now that you have the basics down, it is time to hone your coffee brewing skills and take your brews to the next level. In this chapter, we will dive even deeper into the world of coffee and uncover the secrets to unlocking its true potential. Whether you're a seasoned coffee connoisseur or just beginning your brewing journey, there's always more to learn and explore. So let's roll up our sleeves and discover how to make the best coffee possible.

1. Experiment with Different Coffee Origins: Expand your coffee horizon by trying beans from different regions around the world. Each origin has its unique flavor profile and characteristics, influenced by its soil, climate, altitude, and processing methods. Take a voyage through South America with the nutty and chocolatey flavors of Brazilian coffee, or venture into the bright and floral notes of Ethiopian coffee. By experimenting with different origins, you'll discover new taste experiences and deepen your appreciation for the diverse flavors found in coffee.

To enhance your exploration of coffee origins, consider hosting a coffee cupping session with friends or fellow coffee enthusiasts. Gather a selection of beans from various regions and guide everyone through a tasting experience. Discuss the distinct flavor notes and characteristics of each coffee, encouraging everyone to share their thoughts and preferences. This interactive approach will not only expand your knowledge but also create a fun and engaging atmosphere for everyone involved.

2. Grind Size and Consistency: The grind size of your coffee beans plays a crucial role in the extraction process and ultimately affects the flavor of your brew. Investing in a burr grinder is highly recommended, as it allows for consistent grind size and ensures maximum freshness. Experiment with different grind sizes to find the perfect one for your preferred brewing method. A coarser grind is ideal for methods like the French press, while a finer grind works well for espresso. Take the time to understand the impact of grind size on extraction and adjust it according to your taste preferences.

To further explore the impact of grind size, you can conduct a brewing experiment with a group of friends. Divide the group into smaller teams, with each team using a different grind size for their preferred brewing method. Compare the results and discuss the differences in flavor achieved through varying grind sizes. This hands-on experiment will allow you not only to understand the theory but also to witness the practical effects of grind size firsthand.

Consider using visual aids, such as magnified images or actual samples of coffee grounds under different grind sizes, to help participants visualize the differences. Discuss how finer grinds provide more surface area for extraction, resulting in a stronger and more concentrated flavor, while coarser grinds allow for a slower extraction, resulting in a smoother and milder cup of coffee. This visual demonstration will deepen the participants' understanding of grind size and its impact on flavor.

3. Water Quality and Temperature: The quality of the water you use for brewing plays a significant role in the final taste of your coffee. Investing in a water filtration system, if necessary, is recommended to eliminate impurities that may affect the flavor. Additionally, the water temperature during brewing is crucial. The ideal range for brewing is between 195°F (90°C) and 205°F (96°C). Water that is too hot can result in over-extraction and a bitter taste, while water that is too cold may lead to under-extraction and a weak brew.
4. Brew Time and Ratios: Adjusting your brew time and coffee-to-water ratios can significantly impact the strength and flavor of your coffee. Increasing or decreasing the brew time can subtly alter the extraction, resulting in variations in taste. Similarly, tweaking the coffee-to-water ratios can produce a stronger or milder cup. Keeping a brewing journal will help you track your experiments and find the sweet spot that delights your palate. Remember, brewing coffee is an art, and finding the right balance is key to unlocking its full potential.
5. Pour-Over Techniques: If you enjoy the art of pour-over brewing, consider exploring different techniques like the 'bloom.' This involves pre-wetting the coffee grounds to release trapped gases, allowing for better extraction and a more flavorful cup of coffee. Additionally, experimenting with various pouring patterns can optimize the even saturation of the coffee bed, resulting in a more balanced and nuanced flavor. Try the traditional circular pour, or get creative with a gentle back-and-forth motion to extract different flavor profiles from the coffee grounds.
6. Steaming Milk: If you're a fan of milk-based coffee drinks like lattes or cappuccinos, mastering the art of steaming milk will take your creations to new heights. Pay attention to the texture and temperature of the milk while steaming. The goal is to achieve a velvety smooth microfoam with a temperature around 140°F (60°C). Experiment with different milk varieties like whole milk, oat milk, or almond milk, as they can add unique flavors and textures to your

beverages. Embrace the joy of latte art as you pour the steamed milk into your espresso, creating intricate designs that enhance the visual appeal of your drink.
7. Roasting Your Own Beans: For the adventurous coffee enthusiasts, consider taking your coffee journey a step further by roasting your own beans. This allows you to have complete control over your coffee's flavor profile and freshness. Research different home roasting methods such as hot air roasting or stovetop roasting. As you roast your beans, experiment with different levels of roast, from light to dark, to bring out different flavors and nuances in your coffee. Discover the joy of transforming raw green coffee beans into perfectly roasted gems that create a truly unique cup of coffee.

Now armed with these additional techniques and knowledge, you can elevate your brewing skills and create truly remarkable cups of coffee. Remember, practice makes perfect, so don't be afraid to experiment and adjust your methods to find what works best for your palate. Enjoy the journey of perfecting your coffee brewing skills and savor every sip of your newfound coffee mastery. Happy brewing!

# Chapter 6:
# Tricks and Mistakes to Avoid

In the world of coffee, achieving that perfect cup requires a blend of art and science. To help you on your journey, this chapter offers a comprehensive list of tips and tricks for making successful coffee. Additionally, we'll explore common mistakes that can occur during the brewing process and provide remedies to turn a bad brew into a delightful experience.

## Tips and Tricks for Making Successful Coffee

Brewing a perfect cup of coffee is a rewarding art that combines the right techniques and attention to detail. Whether you're a novice or a seasoned coffee enthusiast, these tips and tricks will help you elevate your coffee game and create consistently excellent brews.

1. Start with Fresh Coffee Beans: Coffee beans have a limited shelf life. The fresher your beans, the better your coffee. Look for beans with a roast date and aim to use them within two to four weeks for optimal flavor.
2. Invest in a Quality Grinder: Grinding your coffee just before brewing is essential for freshness. Invest in a good-quality burr grinder that allows you to adjust the grind size based on your chosen brewing method.

3. Use Clean and Filtered Water: Since coffee is mostly water, the quality of your water matters. Use clean, filtered water without impurities or strong odors. The ideal brewing temperature is around 195-205°F (90-96°C).
4. Measure Coffee and Water Accurately: Consistency is key to great coffee. Use a scale to measure both your coffee grounds and water. This ensures you maintain the proper coffee-to-water ratio for your chosen brewing method.
5. Pre-Wet Coffee Grounds (Blooming): In pour-over and AeroPress brewing, pre-wetting the coffee grounds with a small amount of hot water helps release trapped gases and oils, allowing the coffee to bloom and develop its full flavor.
6. Control Brew Time: Brewing time has a significant impact on your coffee's flavor. Pay attention to the recommended brew time for your method, but don't hesitate to experiment to find the perfect duration for your taste.
7. Keep Your Equipment Clean: Regularly clean your coffee equipment, including grinders, brewers, and filters. Coffee oils and residues can build up over time, affecting the taste of your coffee.
8. Use the Right Grind Size: The grind size you use should match your brewing method. Different methods require different grind sizes to optimize flavor extraction.
9. Store Coffee Properly: Coffee beans are sensitive to light, heat, and moisture. Store your beans in an airtight container, away from direct sunlight, heat sources, and moisture. Avoid the fridge or freezer, as coffee can absorb unwanted odors.
10. Experiment with Water-to-Coffee Ratios: Adjust the coffee-to-water ratio to achieve your preferred strength. While a common guideline is 1 to 2 tablespoons of coffee per 6 ounces of water, you can fine-tune this to suit your taste.

These tips and tricks will help you master the art of coffee brewing. They offer a solid foundation for creating consistently excellent cups of coffee, while also allowing you to explore and refine your own unique coffee-making style. With practice, you'll find the perfect balance that caters to your personal preferences and ensures each cup is a delightful experience.

## Mistakes to Avoid and How to Remedy Them

In the pursuit of brewing a perfect cup of coffee, it's common to encounter a few bumps along the way. Fortunately, many coffee brewing mistakes can be remedied with the right knowledge and adjustments. Here, we'll explore some common errors and how to correct them to ensure your coffee experience remains enjoyable.

1. Over-Extraction

Mistake: Over-extraction occurs when coffee is in contact with hot water for too long, resulting in a bitter and astringent taste.

Remedy:

Shorten the brew time: If you've brewed too long, reduce the steeping time to prevent further extraction.

Use a coarser grind: A coarser grind can help reduce over-extraction, as water passes through the coffee grounds more quickly.

2. Under-Extraction

Mistake: Under-extraction happens when coffee is brewed too quickly, resulting in a sour, weak, and insipid taste.

Remedy:

Extend the brew time: If your coffee is under-extracted, lengthen the brewing time to allow for more flavor extraction.

Use a finer grind: A finer grind can slow down the water flow, improving extraction.

3. Inconsistent Water Temperature

Mistake: Fluctuations in water temperature during brewing can lead to an uneven extraction, resulting in an imbalanced flavor profile.

Remedy:

Use a gooseneck kettle: A kettle with a narrow spout provides better control over the water flow and temperature.

Preheat your equipment: Rinse your brewing equipment with hot water before starting to maintain consistent temperature.

4. Not Using Fresh Beans

Mistake: Stale coffee beans lead to flat and uninspiring brews.

Remedy:

Purchase fresh beans: Look for beans with a recent roast date, and use them within two to four weeks for the best flavor.

Store beans properly: Keep beans in an airtight container in a cool, dark place, away from light, heat, and moisture.

5. Inadequate Grinding

Mistake: Inconsistent or low-quality grinding can result in uneven extraction and subpar flavor.

Remedy:

Invest in a quality grinder: A burr grinder provides consistent grind size and is essential for controlling flavor extraction.

Adjust grind size: Experiment with different grind sizes based on your brewing method.

6. Inaccurate Measurements

Mistake: Guesstimating coffee-to-water ratios can lead to inconsistent results.

Remedy:

Use a scale: Precisely measure both coffee grounds and water to maintain the proper coffee-to-water ratio.

7. Improper Storage

Mistake: Leaving coffee beans exposed to light, heat, and moisture can lead to premature aging and a loss of flavor.

Remedy:

Store beans in an airtight container: Keep your beans in a container that prevents exposure to air and light.

Avoid the fridge or freezer: Coffee can absorb unwanted odors in the fridge or freezer, so store it in a cool, dark place.

By recognizing these common coffee brewing mistakes and learning how to correct them, you can enjoy a more consistent and delightful coffee experience. The journey of mastering coffee brewing involves continuous experimentation and refinement, and these remedies will guide you toward that perfect cup you've been aiming to create.

# Chapter 7:
# Coffee Recipes Around the World

Welcome to "Coffee Around the World!" In this chapter, we will embark on a global journey to discover the diverse and unique flavors of coffee from around the world. With 50 delightful recipes, we will explore the rich cultural traditions and brewing techniques that make each country's coffee experience so special. From Espresso Martini and Vietnamese Egg Coffee to familiar favorites such as Irish Coffee and American Pumpkin Spice Latte, this chapter is sure to awaken your taste buds and expand your coffee horizons. So grab your favorite mug, sit back, and prepare to embark on an aromatic adventure through the enticing world of international coffee recipes.

# Espresso Martini

**Ingredient List:**
- 2 oz (60 ml) vodka
- 1 oz (30 ml) coffee liqueur
- 1 oz (30 ml) freshly brewed espresso
- 1/2 oz (15 ml) simple syrup
- Ice cubes

**Preparation time**: 5 minutes
**Portion Information**: Makes 1 serving
**Equipment Tips:** It is recommended to use a cocktail shaker, a jigger or measuring cup, and a martini glass for the best presentation.

**Instructions:**
1. Begin by chilling your martini glass. Simply place it in the freezer for a few minutes while you prepare the cocktail.
2. In a cocktail shaker, add the vodka, coffee liqueur, freshly brewed espresso, and simple syrup. Make sure to measure accurately for a balanced and flavorful cocktail.
3. Fill the shaker with ice cubes. The ice will not only chill the ingredients but also dilute the cocktail slightly, balancing the flavors.
4. Firmly close the shaker and shake vigorously for about 15 seconds. This will create a frothy texture and blend all the ingredients together harmoniously.
5. Retrieve your chilled martini glass from the freezer and strain the contents of the shaker into the glass. The fine strainer on your shaker will help keep any ice shards or excess foam from the cocktail.
6. For an added touch of sophistication, you can garnish the Espresso Martini with a few coffee beans on top. This not only looks aesthetically pleasing but also gives a hint of the flavors to come.
7. Serve your Espresso Martini immediately and enjoy it while it's still cold. The rich coffee flavor, the smoothness of the vodka, and the sweetness of the coffee liqueur will unite in a delightful and invigorating sip.

Cheers to a delectable Espresso Martini! Let its intricate blend of flavors and the sheer joy of sipping it transport you to a world infused with culinary artistry.

# Turkish Coffee

**Ingredient List:**
- Turkish coffee - 1.5 ounces (40 grams)
- Cold water - 6 fluid ounces (180 milliliters)
- Sugar (optional) - to taste

**Preparation time**: 10 minutes
**Portion Information**: This recipe makes one serving.

**Equipment Tips:**
For the best results, it is recommended to use a traditional Turkish coffee pot called a cezve. However, if you don't have one, a small saucepan will work as a substitute. Additionally, a coffee grinder is needed to grind the coffee beans to a fine powder.

**Instructions:**
1. Start by grinding the Turkish coffee beans to a fine powder consistency. It's essential for achieving the desired texture and flavor. Aim for a consistency similar to powdered sugar.
2. Measure out 6 fluid ounces (180 milliliters) of cold water. The ratio of coffee to water is crucial in Turkish coffee, so make sure to keep the measurements accurate.
3. Transfer the ground Turkish coffee into the cezve or small saucepan, along with the measured cold water. If desired, you can add sugar at this point, depending on your taste preferences. Keep in mind that traditional Turkish coffee is usually prepared without sugar.
4. Place the cezve or saucepan on low heat. Slowly and gently stir the mixture with a spoon until the coffee begins to dissolve. Do not use any excessive force while stirring, as you don't want to create bubbles or froth.
5. Increase the heat to medium-low, but do not let it boil. Allow the coffee to heat up gradually. Keep an eye on it to prevent overheating.
6. As the coffee starts to heat up, a thick foam layer will gradually form on top. This is an essential part of Turkish coffee. When the foam reaches the edge of the pot, carefully remove the cezve or saucepan from the heat. Stir the foam briefly and return it to the heat.
7. Repeat the process in step 6 three times. This will help to enhance the richness and aroma of the coffee. Once the foam reaches the edge for the fourth time, it's ready.
8. Remove the cezve or saucepan from the heat completely. Let it sit for a brief moment to allow the grounds to settle.
9. Pour the Turkish coffee into small espresso cups, leaving behind the sediment at the bottom of the cezve or saucepan. Serve immediately.
10. Enjoy the unique experience of sipping on this strong and aromatic Turkish coffee. Take small sips, allowing the flavors to linger on your tastebuds. It is especially delightful when accompanied by a glass of cold water to cleanse your palate.

Note: Turkish coffee is typically served without milk or cream. If desired, you can serve it with a small piece of Turkish delight or any traditional sweet treat as an accompaniment.

Remember, preparing Turkish coffee is not only about making a beverage but also an ancient art form that brings people together to share in the joy of coffee appreciation. Take your time, embrace the process, and savor each sip of this delightful Turkish tradition.

## Ethiopian Coffee Ceremony

**Ingredient List:**
- Ethiopian Coffee beans - 2 ounces (56 grams)
- Water - 8 cups (1.89 liters)
- Sugar - to taste (optional)

**Preparation time**: 30 minutes
**Portion Information**: Serves 4-6 people

**Equipment Tips:** Traditional Ethiopian coffee ceremony equipment includes:
- Jebena (coffee pot)
- Buna Buna (a special stove or charcoal cooker)
- Fenjal (clay or stone cups)

**Instructions:**
1. Begin by roasting the coffee beans. Heat a skillet over medium heat and add the coffee beans. Continuously stir the beans using a wooden spoon to ensure even roasting. The beans will darken and release their aromatic oils. Roast for about 15 minutes, or until the beans turn a rich brown color. Be careful not to burn them.
2. Grind the roasted coffee beans using a mortar and pestle or a coffee grinder until you achieve a fine consistency. The smell of freshly ground coffee will fill the air, intensifying your anticipation.
3. Fill the Jebena with water by carefully pouring it into the narrow top opening. Place the Jebena on the Buna Buna stove or charcoal cooker, and let the water come to a gentle boil. The unique design of the Jebena ensures that the water being heated is separate from the coffee grounds.
4. Once the water is boiling, remove the Jebena from the heat. Add the finely ground coffee directly into the water, allowing it to float on top. Do not stir.
5. Place the Jebena back on the heat source and let the coffee steep for a few minutes. The aroma will fill the room, creating an inviting atmosphere.
6. Pour a small amount of coffee into the Fenjal cups, creating a layer of crema on top. This process should be repeated three times to ensure the maximum extraction of flavor.

7. Serve the coffee using the traditional Ethiopian Coffee Ceremony technique: hold the Fenjal cup from the bottom and serve it to each guest. The host should serve the eldest guest first, and then proceed in order of age.
8. Ethiopian coffee is often served without sugar, but you can adjust the sweetness to your liking by adding sugar to each cup, if desired.
9. Encourage your guests to enjoy the coffee slowly, savoring the flavors and taking part in the joyous and social experience of the Ethiopian Coffee Ceremony.

Embrace the artistry of this beautiful Ethiopian Coffee Ceremony and delight in the rich flavors and cultural traditions it brings.

## French Vanilla Latte

**Ingredient List:**
- 1 shot of espresso (30 ml, 1 ounce)
- 1 cup of whole milk (240 ml, 8.12 ounces)
- 1 tablespoon of vanilla syrup (15 ml, 0.51 ounces)
- Whipped cream (optional, for garnish)
- Ground cinnamon (optional, for garnish)

**Preparation time**: 10 minutes

**Portion Information**: Makes 1 serving

**Equipment Tips:**
- Espresso machine or espresso maker
- Steaming pitcher
- Milk thermometer
- Coffee mug
- Whisk or spoon for stirring
- Electric milk frother (optional)
- Handheld milk frother (optional)

**Instructions:**
1. Start by brewing a shot of espresso using an espresso machine or espresso maker. Ensure that the espresso has a rich and smooth flavor.
2. In a steaming pitcher, add the whole milk. Heat the milk using a steam wand or on a stovetop until it reaches around 150°F (65°C). This temperature creates a creamy texture and enhances the sweetness of the milk.
3. If you prefer frothed milk, you can use an electric or handheld milk frother to create a velvety foam. Froth the milk until it reaches your desired consistency.
4. Pour the vanilla syrup into a coffee mug. If you enjoy a pronounced vanilla flavor, you can add an extra teaspoon of syrup.

5. Carefully pour the shot of espresso into the mug over the vanilla syrup. Stir gently with a whisk or spoon to combine the flavors.
6. Slowly pour the steamed milk into the mug, allowing it to blend with the espresso and vanilla syrup. Hold back the foam with a spoon and gradually release it to the top.
7. If desired, top your French Vanilla Latte with a dollop of whipped cream. Sprinkle a pinch of ground cinnamon on top for a touch of warmth and aroma.
8. Serve the French Vanilla Latte immediately, while it's still hot. Savor the creamy texture, the fragrant vanilla, and the rich espresso notes. Enjoy!

Note: Feel free to adjust the sweetness of your latte by adding more or less vanilla syrup according to your preference. Additionally, if you don't have an espresso machine, you can use a strong batch of brewed coffee as a substitute for the espresso shot.

# Italian Hazelnut Espresso

**Ingredient List:**
- Freshly ground espresso beans - 1 ounce (28 grams)
- Roasted hazelnuts - 1 tablespoon (15 grams)
- Milk - 6 ounces (180 milliliters)
- Hazelnut syrup - 1 tablespoon (15 milliliters)
- Chocolate syrup - 1 tablespoon (15 milliliters)

**Preparation time**: 10 minutes
**Portion Information**: 1 serving
**Equipment Tips:**
- Espresso machine or coffee maker
- Coffee grinder (for grinding espresso beans)
- Milk frother or steam wand
- Small saucepan
- Stirring spoon

**Instructions:**
1. Start by grinding 1 ounce (28 grams) of freshly roasted espresso beans to a fine texture using a coffee grinder.
2. Place the ground espresso into the portafilter of your espresso machine or coffee maker. Tamp down gently to ensure an even extraction.
3. Brew the espresso according to the instructions of your machine, making sure to extract around 1 ounce (30 milliliters) of rich and aromatic espresso.
4. While your espresso is brewing, pour 6 ounces (180 milliliters) of milk into a small saucepan. Heat the milk on low heat until it reaches a temperature of around 150°F (65°C), ensuring it doesn't boil.

5. Once the milk is heated, use a milk frother or steam wand to create a velvety and creamy foam. Hold the frother slightly tilted to create a whirlpool effect while steaming.
6. Toast the hazelnuts in a dry skillet over medium heat for a few minutes, until they become golden and fragrant. Remove them from the skillet and crush them into small pieces.
7. In a coffee cup or mug, combine 1 tablespoon (15 milliliters) of hazelnut syrup and 1 tablespoon (15 milliliters) of chocolate syrup.
8. Pour the freshly brewed espresso over the syrups, and give it a gentle stir to combine.
9. Slowly pour the steamed milk over the espresso, holding back the foam with a spoon.
10. Top the hazelnut espresso with a generous layer of milk foam, creating beautiful latte art if desired.
11. Sprinkle the crushed toasted hazelnuts on top of the foam for an extra nutty flavor and visual appeal.
12. Serve the Italian Hazelnut Espresso immediately and enjoy the harmonious blend of rich espresso, creamy foam, and indulgent hazelnut and chocolate syrups.

Embrace the artistry of this Italian Hazelnut Espresso, where the boldness of freshly ground espresso meets the nutty-sweet notes of roasted hazelnuts. Each sip will transport you to the enchanting streets of Italy, where passion for coffee intertwines with a flair for culinary elegance. Indulge in the symphony of flavors and embrace the mastery of the barista within you. Buon appetito!

# Moroccan Spiced Coffee

**Ingredient List:**
- Ground coffee - 2 ounces (56 grams)
- Ground cardamom - 1 teaspoon (2 grams)
- Ground cinnamon - 1 teaspoon (2 grams)
- Ground ginger - 1/2 teaspoon (1 gram)
- Ground nutmeg - 1/2 teaspoon (1 gram)
- Ground cloves - 1/4 teaspoon (0.5 gram)
- Water - 16 fluid ounces (473 ml)
- Milk - 8 fluid ounces (237 ml)
- Honey or sugar - to taste

**Preparation time**: 15 minutes
**Portion Information**: 2 servings
**Equipment Tips:**
- Coffee grinder: Use a coffee grinder to freshly grind the whole coffee beans for a more flavorful cup of coffee.
- Stovetop pot: A small saucepan or pot will be perfect for brewing the coffee.

**Instructions:**

1. Start by grinding the whole coffee beans to a medium-fine consistency. Aim for a texture similar to granulated sugar.
2. In a small bowl, combine the ground coffee, cardamom, cinnamon, ginger, nutmeg, and cloves. Mix them well to ensure even distribution of the spices.
3. Pour the water into a stovetop pot and add the spice and coffee mixture. Give it a gentle stir to moisten all the grounds.
4. Place the pot over medium heat and let it come to a gentle simmer. Avoid boiling the coffee as it can result in a more bitter taste.
5. Once the coffee starts to simmer, reduce the heat to low and let it brew for about 10 minutes. During this time, the aroma of the spices will infuse into the coffee, creating a delightful fragrance.
6. While the coffee is brewing, heat the milk in a separate pot or microwave until steaming hot but not boiling.
7. Once the coffee has brewed, remove it from the heat and let it rest for a minute to allow the coffee grounds to settle to the bottom.
8. Carefully pour the brewed coffee through a fine-mesh sieve or coffee filter into serving cups or mugs. This step will help remove any remaining coffee grounds and provide a smoother texture.
9. Add the steamed milk to the cups, pouring it slowly to create a beautiful layered effect. Stir gently to incorporate the coffee and milk.
10. Sweeten your Moroccan Spiced Coffee with honey or sugar according to your taste preference. Start with a teaspoon and adjust as needed.
11. Serve immediately and enjoy the aromatic and exotic flavors of Moroccan Spiced Coffee!

Note: Feel free to experiment with the spice proportions and adjust them to your personal taste. Additionally, you can garnish the coffee with a sprinkle of ground cinnamon or nutmeg for an extra touch of elegance.

# Australian Flat White

**Ingredient List:**
- 2 shots of espresso (2 fl oz / 60 ml)
- 6 fl oz of milk (180 ml)

**Preparation time**: 10 minutes

**Portion Information**: 1 serving.
**Equipment Tips:**
To make the perfect Australian Flat White, you will need a coffee machine with an

espresso function, a frothing pitcher, and a flat white cup or mug.

Detailed instructions for preparation and cooking:
1. Grind your coffee beans to a fine consistency suitable for espresso brewing. Use approximately 18-20 grams of coffee beans for a double shot.
2. Tamp the coffee grounds firmly into the portafilter to ensure an even extraction. Lock the portafilter into the espresso machine.
3. Preheat your coffee machine by running water through the group head without the portafilter attached. This will ensure the cup is properly warmed.
4. Place a preheated flat white cup or mug underneath the portafilter and start the extraction by pressing the appropriate button on your espresso machine. Aim to extract 2 fluid ounces (60 ml) of espresso, which should take about 20-30 seconds.
5. While the espresso is brewing, take the milk and pour it into a frothing pitcher. Use fresh, cold milk for the best results.
6. Purge the steam wand by releasing a small amount of steam to remove any condensed water before frothing the milk.
7. Place the steam wand just below the surface of the milk and turn on the steam. Gradually lower the pitcher to keep the steam wand at the same level as the milk.
8. Froth the milk by positioning the steam wand at an angle, creating a whirlpool effect. Make sure to introduce enough air into the milk to achieve a silky and velvety texture, but avoid large bubbles.
9. Once the milk reaches a temperature of around 150°F (65°C), turn off the steam wand and wipe it clean with a damp cloth.
10. Gently tap the milk pitcher on the counter to dissipate any remaining bubbles and swirl the milk to achieve a smooth consistency.
11. Begin pouring the frothed milk into the espresso, aiming to create intricate latte art patterns.
12. Finally, marvel at your culinary masterpiece and enjoy the smooth, velvety Australian Flat White immediately.

Note: The art of creating a perfect Australian Flat White lies in achieving a balanced ratio of espresso to milk. The resulting drink should feature a rich, velvety texture with a perfect harmony between the bold flavor of the espresso and the creamy sweetness of the milk. Experiment with different beans, milk ratios, and milk frothing techniques to find your ideal balance.

# Greek Honey Frappé

**Ingredient List:**
- 2 tsp (10 gr) instant coffee
- 4 tsp (20 gr) granulated sugar
- 2/3 cup (150 ml) cold water
- 4-6 ice cubes
- 1/2 cup (120 ml) whole milk
- 2 tbsp (30 ml) Greek honey
- Whipped cream (optional)
- Cinnamon powder (optional)

**Preparation time**: 10 minutes
**Portion Information**: Serves 1
**Equipment Tips:**
- Blender or shaker
- Tall glass

**Instructions:**
1. In a blender or shaker, combine the instant coffee, sugar, and water. If using a blender, pulse for about 10 seconds until the mixture becomes frothy. If using a shaker, vigorously shake for about 20 seconds.
2. Fill a tall glass with ice cubes and pour the frothy coffee mixture over the ice.
3. Slowly pour the milk into the glass, allowing it to mix with the coffee as it settles.
4. Drizzle the Greek honey over the top of the frothy coffee and milk mixture.
5. (Optional) Gently swirl the glass to combine the ingredients or use a spoon to stir without disturbing the foam.
6. If desired, top the frappé with a dollop of whipped cream and sprinkle some cinnamon powder for additional flavor and presentation.
7. Serve immediately and enjoy the refreshing and indulgent Greek Honey Frappé.

# Cuban Café Con Miel

**Ingredient List:**
- 2 ounces (60 ml) of freshly brewed Cuban coffee
- 1 tablespoon (15 ml) of honey
- 2 ounces (60 ml) of milk

**Preparation time**: 10 minutes

**Portion Information:** Serves 1

**Equipment Tips:** Use a stove-top espresso maker or a French press for brewing the coffee. A small saucepan and a frother or whisk will be needed for heating and frothing the milk.

**Instructions:**
1. Brew a strong cup of Cuban coffee using your preferred method. Make sure to use high-quality coffee beans for a rich and authentic flavor.
2. In a small saucepan, warm the milk over medium heat until it begins to steam. Avoid boiling it.
3. Froth the milk using a frother or whisk. Aim for a velvety consistency and creamy texture.
4. In a heatproof cup, combine the brewed coffee and honey. Stir until the honey is fully dissolved.
5. Slowly pour the frothed milk into the cup, aiming for beautiful latte art or a consistent layer of foam.
6. Serve immediately and enjoy the delightful combination of strong Cuban coffee, sweet honey, and creamy milk.

Note: Feel free to adjust the amount of honey and milk according to your taste preferences. Some may prefer a sweeter or stronger coffee, while others may prefer more or less milk. Experiment to find your perfect balance.

Embrace the allure of Cuban Café Con Miel as it tantalizes your taste buds and brings you closer to the vibrant culture of Cuba. Savor each sip and indulge in the artistry of this delectable beverage. ¡Buen provecho!

# Italian Affogato

**Ingredient List:**
- 2 shots (3.5 fl oz or 100 ml) of hot espresso
- 4 scoops (8.8 oz or 250 gr) of high-quality vanilla gelato

**Preparation time**: 5 minutes

**Portion Information**: Serves 2

**Equipment Tips:**
- Espresso machine or coffee maker
- Ice cream scoop
- Heatproof glasses or cups

**Instructions:**
1. Prepare 2 shots of hot espresso using an espresso machine or coffee maker. Make sure the espresso is robust and aromatic, as it forms the base of this delightful dessert.
2. While the espresso is brewing, take out 2 heatproof glasses or cups for serving the affogato. It's essential to use heatproof glassware because the hot espresso will be poured over the cold gelato.
3. Take 4 generous scoops of high-quality vanilla gelato using an ice cream scoop. The velvety smoothness and subtle sweetness of the gelato perfectly complement the strong flavor of the espresso.
4. Place two scoops of gelato into each serving glass. Make sure they are nicely rounded, enticing the visual senses with their creamy texture.
5. Pour one shot of hot espresso over each scoop of gelato. The hot espresso cascading over the cold gelato creates a mesmerizing spectacle, highlighting the harmony of temperature contrasts.
6. Allow the affogato to sit for a brief moment, allowing the flavors to meld together and the gelato to slightly melt. This delicate blending of hot and cold is a testament to the artistry of Italian cuisine.
7. Serve the Italian Affogato immediately and marvel at the simplicity yet sophistication of this dessert. Encourage your guests to indulge in this harmonious marriage of robust coffee flavors and luscious gelato textures.

Indulge in the allure of Italian culinary artistry with this sensational Italian Affogato recipe. Immerse yourself in the sensory experience it offers, from the aromatic coffee aroma to the velvety gelato melting on your tongue—a true masterpiece that combines simplicity, elegance, and flavor.

# Indian Filter Coffee

**Ingredient List:**
- 2 tablespoons (30 ml) finely ground Indian coffee
- 1 cup (240 ml) water
- 2 tablespoons (30 ml) milk
- 1 teaspoon (5 ml) sugar (optional)

**Preparation time**: 10 minutes
**Portion Information**: Makes 1 serving
**Equipment Tips:**
- Indian Filter Coffee Maker: This unique brewing device is essential for achieving the true flavor of Indian filter coffee. Its unique design allows for the coffee to steep and drip slowly, resulting in a rich and aromatic cup of coffee.
- Coffee Grinder: Invest in a good quality grinder to ensure a consistent and fine grind, which is crucial for the perfect cup of Indian filter coffee.

**Instructions:**
1. Begin by grinding your Indian coffee beans to a fine consistency. The aroma released during this process will transport you to the bustling streets of India.
2. Pour water into the lower chamber of the Indian Filter Coffee Maker. Place the filter disc on top of the water chamber.
3. Add the ground coffee to the filter disc and gently tap it to create an even bed of coffee. Smooth and precise movements are essential in the art of brewing.
4. Slowly pour hot water onto the coffee bed using a circular motion. The water should be just below boiling point. Allow the coffee to bloom and release its flavors for a few minutes.
5. Now, attach the upper chamber of the filter maker and cover it with the lid. Let the magic happen as the coffee slowly drips down into the lower chamber.
6. While the coffee is brewing, warm the milk in a separate container. Remember, the milk should be hot, but not boiling.
7. Once the brewing process is complete, mix the freshly brewed coffee and the hot milk in equal proportions. For a sweeter taste, add a teaspoon of sugar or adjust according to your preference.
8. Now, relish the enticing aroma and flavors of your homemade Indian Filter Coffee. Sip it slowly and savor the unique taste that only this traditional method can produce.

Sit back, relax, and enjoy your authentic cup of Indian Filter Coffee. Let the warmth and depth of flavors transport you to the vibrant streets of India.

# Moroccan Mint Coffee

**Ingredient List:**
- 2 tablespoons (30 ml) freshly ground coffee
- 3 cups (710 ml) water
- 1/4 cup (50 grams) sugar
- 1/4 cup (60 ml) hot water
- 1 bunch fresh mint leaves
- Ice cubes

**Preparation time**: 15 minutes
**Portion Information**: 4 servings
**Equipment Tips:**
- Medium-sized saucepan
- Coffee filter or French press
- Mugs or glasses for serving
- Fine mesh strainer

**Instructions:**
1. Begin by boiling the water in a medium-sized saucepan. Once the water comes to a boil, remove it from the heat.
2. Add the freshly ground coffee into the boiling water and let it steep for about 5 minutes. This will allow the flavors to infuse into the coffee.
3. While the coffee is steeping, dissolve the sugar in a separate 1/4 cup of hot water. Stir it until the sugar dissolves completely.
4. Take your bunch of fresh mint leaves and gently crush them to release their aroma and flavor. You can do this by rubbing them together between your hands.
5. Once the coffee has finished steeping, strain it through a fine mesh strainer to remove the coffee grounds. Discard the grounds and return the strained coffee to the saucepan.
6. Pour the dissolved sugar mixture into the coffee and stir well to combine.
7. Add the crushed mint leaves into the coffee and let it steep for an additional 5 minutes. This will infuse the coffee with the refreshing mint flavor.
8. After the mint has steeped, strain the coffee once more to remove the mint leaves. Again, discard the leaves and transfer the flavored coffee to a separate container.
9. Place the coffee in the refrigerator to chill for at least 2 hours. This will ensure that it is cold and refreshing when served.
10. When ready to serve, fill each glass with ice cubes and pour the chilled Moroccan Mint Coffee over the ice.
11. Garnish each glass with a sprig of fresh mint leaves for an extra touch of elegance.
12. Enjoy your Moroccan Mint Coffee as a delightful and invigorating beverage to start your day or as a refreshing treat to unwind in the afternoon.

# Chinese Yuenyeung

**Ingredient List:**
- Strong black tea - 4 oz (120 ml)
- Freshly brewed coffee - 2 oz (60 ml)
- Sweetened condensed milk - 2 tbsp (30 ml)
- Evaporated milk - 2 tbsp (30 ml)
- Ice cubes - as desired

**Preparation time**: 10 minutes

**Portion Information**: 1 serving

**Equipment Tips:**
- Brew the tea and coffee separately using a teapot and a coffee maker or French press.
- Use a tall glass to serve the Yuenyeung to showcase its beautiful layered colors.

**Instructions:**
1. Start by brewing a strong black tea. Use a teapot to steep the tea leaves in boiling water for about 5 minutes. Strain the tea and set it aside to cool.
2. While the tea is cooling, brew a fresh cup of coffee using your preferred method. Make sure the coffee is strong and aromatic, as it will contribute to the unique flavor of Yuenyeung.
3. In a tall glass, add the cooled black tea first, filling it halfway. Then, gently pour the freshly brewed coffee over the tea to create a distinct separation between the two layers. Marvel at the mesmerizing visual contrast!
4. Next, drizzle 1 tablespoon of sweetened condensed milk over the coffee layer. This will add a touch of sweetness and richness to your Yuenyeung.
5. Finally, top it off with 1 tablespoon of evaporated milk. The evaporated milk adds creaminess and balances the flavors of tea and coffee harmoniously.
6. Add ice cubes to the glass, allowing the Yuenyeung to cool further and become refreshingly cold.
7. Grab a stirring stick or a long spoon and give the Yuenyeung a gentle stir to blend the layers slightly, enhancing the flavor fusion while maintaining its attractive appearance.
8. Serve immediately and enjoy this delightful Chinese Yuenyeung, where the boldness of black tea and the robustness of coffee intertwine in a symphony of taste and visual appeal!
9. Pro Tip: Feel free to adjust the proportions of tea, coffee, and milk according to your personal preference. Some like it sweeter, while others prefer a stronger tea or coffee flavor. Experiment and find your perfect Yuenyeung balance!

Note: Chinese Yuenyeung can be enjoyed as a hot or cold beverage, depending on your preference.

# French Café au Lait

**Ingredient List:**
- Strong brewed coffee - 6 ounces (180 ml)
- Milk - 6 ounces (180 ml)

**Preparation time**: 10 minutes

**Portion Information**: 1 serving

**Equipment Tips:**
- Coffee maker or French press
- Milk frother or small saucepan

**Instructions:**
1. Start by brewing a strong pot of coffee using your favorite coffee maker or prepare it using a French press. We want a bold and flavorful base for our Café au Lait.
2. While the coffee is brewing, heat the milk. If you have a milk frother, use it to froth the milk until it becomes velvety and airy. If you don't have a frother, no worries! You can heat the milk in a small saucepan over low heat until it steams and then whisk vigorously to create some foam.
3. Once the coffee is brewed and the milk is ready, it's time to combine them in a beautiful harmony. Slowly pour the coffee into a large mug, filling it halfway.
4. Next, pour the frothed milk over the coffee, allowing it to mix gently. The creamy milk should create a captivating swirl pattern on the surface of your Café au Lait.
5. Take a moment to appreciate the exquisite aroma and the inviting appearance of your creation. The combination of strong coffee and creamy milk is what sets this French specialty apart.
6. Serve your Café au Lait immediately, savoring each sip as you indulge in the beauty of this classic French beverage. Its smoothness and gentle elegance are perfect to enjoy during a quiet morning, or as an afternoon pick-me-up.

Cheers to the artistry of culinary delights. Bon appétit!

# Spanish Cortado

**Ingredient List:**
- 1 shot (1.5 oz, 45 ml) of espresso
- Equal parts (1.5 oz, 45 ml) of warm milk

**Preparation time**: 5 minutes

**Portion Information**: 1 serving

**Equipment Tips:**
- Espresso machine
- Milk frother or steam wand

Detailed instructions for preparation and cooking:
1. Start by brewing a shot of espresso using an espresso machine. If you don't have one at hand, you can also use a stovetop moka pot or a French press to make a strong coffee concentrate.
2. While the espresso is brewing, warm the milk by using a milk frother or the steam wand of your espresso machine. Heat it until it reaches a temperature of around 150°F (65°C). Make sure not to overheat the milk, as it can affect its taste and texture.
3. Once the espresso is ready, pour it into a small cup or glass.
4. Now, it's time to create the perfect balance. Gently pour the warm milk into the cup, allowing it to mix with the espresso. The amount of milk should be equal to the amount of espresso, creating a harmonious fusion.
5. Take a moment to appreciate the contrasting colors as the rich, dark espresso swirls with the creamy, light milk, creating an enticing visual display.
6. Now, it's time to enjoy your Spanish Cortado. Take a sip and relish the unique blend of flavors. Notice how the intensity of the espresso is softened by the velvety texture of the milk, resulting in a smooth, rounded taste.
7. Embrace the ritual of savoring your Cortado slowly. Allow the flavors to dance on your palate and stimulate your senses.

Remember, the Spanish Cortado is more than just a coffee beverage; it embodies the essence of Spain's coffee culture. So, take your time and indulge in this culinary artwork that combines the technique of espresso brewing with the artistry of milk steaming. Buen provecho!

# Mexican Café de Olla

**Ingredient List:**
- 4 ounces (115g) medium grind coffee
- 4 cups (950ml) water
- 1 cinnamon stick
- 1 whole clove
- 2 tablespoons (30ml) piloncillo (unrefined cane sugar)
- 1 orange peel

**Preparation time**: 30 minutes
**Portion Information:** 4 servings.
**Equipment Tips:**
- Coffee grinder
- Saucepan
- Wooden spoon
- Strainer

**Instructions:**
1. Start by grinding your coffee beans to a medium grind consistency. This will ensure the perfect extraction of flavors without any bitter notes. Use a coffee grinder for the best results.
2. In a saucepan over medium heat, add the water and bring it to a gentle simmer.
3. Once the water is simmering, add the cinnamon stick, whole clove, piloncillo, and orange peel. These aromatic ingredients will infuse the coffee with delightful flavors.
4. Stir the mixture gently with a wooden spoon, ensuring that the piloncillo dissolves completely. Let it simmer for about 15 minutes to allow the spices and sugar to meld together.
5. After 15 minutes, add the ground coffee to the saucepan. Stir it gently to ensure that all the coffee grounds are wet and distributed evenly.
6. Continue to simmer the coffee for another 5 minutes, stirring occasionally. This slow and gentle simmer will extract the rich flavors from the coffee beans, creating a delicious brew.
7. Turn off the heat and let the Café de Olla sit for a couple of minutes to allow the coffee grounds to settle at the bottom of the saucepan.
8. Carefully pour the Café de Olla through a strainer into individual coffee cups or mugs. This will remove any remaining coffee grounds or other solids, ensuring a smooth and satisfying cup of coffee.
9. Serve your Mexican Café de Olla hot and enjoy the intricate flavors of cinnamon, orange, and piloncillo dancing with the rich coffee notes.

Embrace the delightful tradition of Mexican Café de Olla and savor the magical combination of flavors that make this beverage a true work of art.

# Irish Coffee

**Ingredient List:**
- 1.5 oz (45 ml) Irish whiskey
- 2 tsp (10g) brown sugar
- 4 oz (120 ml) hot strong coffee
- 1 oz (30 ml) heavy cream

**Preparation time**: 10 minutes
**Portion Information**: Makes 1 serving
**Equipment Tips:** It is recommended to use a heatproof glass or mug for serving.

**Instructions:**
1. Begin by heating your glass or mug with hot water. This will ensure that your Irish Coffee stays warm for longer.
2. In a separate glass or bowl, measure out the Irish whiskey and brown sugar. Stir until the sugar has fully dissolved.
3. Brew a strong cup of coffee using your preferred method. Ensure that the coffee is hot.
4. Empty the heated glass or mug and pour in the prepared whiskey and sugar mixture.
5. Fill the glass or mug about three-quarters full with the hot coffee. Stir gently to combine.
6. In a separate small container, pour in the heavy cream. With the backside of a spoon, slowly pour the cream onto the back of the spoon, allowing it to float on top of the coffee.
7. Serve the Irish Coffee immediately while still hot.

Enjoy the delightful combination of Irish whiskey, coffee, and creamy goodness in this classic drink that will warm your soul and elevate your senses.

# South Korean Dalgona Coffee

**Ingredient List:**
- Instant coffee - 2 tablespoons (10g)
- White granulated sugar - 2 tablespoons (25g)
- Hot water - 2 tablespoons (30ml)
- Milk - 1 cup (240ml)
- Ice cubes (optional)

**Preparation time**: 15 minutes
**Portion Information**: Makes 1 serving
**Equipment Tips:**
- Mixing bowl
- Whisk or electric mixer
- Tall glass or coffee mug

Detailed instructions for preparation and cooking:
1. In a mixing bowl, combine the instant coffee, sugar, and hot water. Make sure to use equal parts of each ingredient.
2. Using a whisk or electric mixer, vigorously whip the mixture for about 5-10 minutes. You can also do this by hand, but it will take a bit longer. The mixture should start to lighten in color and thicken into a creamy foam.
3. While you continue whisking, heat the milk in a saucepan or microwave until hot but not boiling. If desired, add a pinch of sugar to the milk for a touch of sweetness.
4. Once the coffee mixture has reached a frothy consistency and the milk is hot, you are ready to assemble your Dalgona coffee.
5. Fill a tall glass or coffee mug with ice cubes (if using) and pour in the milk, leaving a little room at the top.
6. Carefully spoon the whipped coffee on top of the milk, allowing it to sit on the surface. You can create beautiful designs or shapes with the whipped coffee by swirling it around gently.
7. Serve immediately and be sure to mix the whipped coffee into the milk before sipping to enjoy the full flavor. You can use a spoon or a straw for this delightful process.
8. Sit back, savor the moment, and experience the rich, creamy, and velvety South Korean Dalgona Coffee at its finest.

Enjoy!

# Finnish Kaffeost

**Ingredient List:**
- 8 ounces (225 grams) of Finnish squeaky cheese
- 4 cups (960 milliliters) of strong black coffee

**Preparation time**: 10 minutes
**Portion Information**: 4 servings
**Equipment Tips:** For best results, use a non-stick frying pan and a French press or espresso machine.

**Instructions:**
1. Begin by preheating a non-stick frying pan over medium heat. While the pan is heating, slice the Finnish squeaky cheese into thin, rectangular pieces.
2. Once the pan is hot, place the cheese slices in a single layer and allow them to heat through. Be patient and attentive, as the cheese will start to soften and develop a golden-brown crust. This process should take approximately 5 minutes.
3. While the cheese is browning, prepare your strong black coffee. Brew your coffee using a French press or an espresso machine, whichever you prefer. Ensure that the coffee is full-bodied and has a robust flavor.
4. Once the cheese slices have developed a satisfying crust, carefully remove them from the pan with a spatula and place them on individual serving plates.
5. Next, pour the hot black coffee over the crispy cheese slices, allowing the flavors to meld together harmoniously.
6. Serve immediately and enjoy the unique experience of savoring the Finnish Kaffeost. As you sip the coffee and bite into the warm, softened cheese, relish the contrasting textures and flavors that truly make this dish a culinary masterpiece.

Note: Finnish Kaffeost is traditionally consumed by picking up the cheese slices with your fingers and sipping the coffee between bites. Embrace the tactile and sensory experience as you indulge in this delightful Scandinavian delicacy.
Bon appétit!

# Jamaican Blue Mountain Coffee

**Ingredient List:**
- Jamaican Blue Mountain coffee beans - 2 ounces (56 grams)
- Water - 16 ounces (473 milliliters)

**Preparation time**: 10 minutes

**Portion Information**: 1 cup

**Equipment Tips:** Use a coffee grinder, French press, and stovetop kettle for the best results.

**Instructions:**
1. Begin by measuring out 2 ounces (56 grams) of Jamaican Blue Mountain coffee beans. These beans are renowned for their exceptional quality, offering a smooth and vibrant flavor profile.
2. Heat 16 ounces (473 milliliters) of water in a stovetop kettle. Fresh, filtered water is recommended to ensure the purest taste in your coffee.
3. While the water is heating, grind the coffee beans to a medium coarseness using a coffee grinder. This will allow for optimal extraction of flavors during the brewing process.
4. Once the water has reached a temperature just below boiling point (around 200°F or 93°C), pour it over the ground coffee in a French press. It's crucial to use the right water temperature, as excessively hot water can result in a bitter taste.
5. Stir the coffee and water mixture gently and let it steep for about 4 minutes. This steeping process allows the flavors to fully develop, yielding a rich and aromatic cup of coffee.
6. After the steeping time has passed, press the plunger of the French press slowly down, separating the brewed coffee from the grounds. This step ensures a clean and sediment-free cup of coffee.
7. Pour the freshly brewed Jamaican Blue Mountain Coffee into a preheated cup and savor its exquisite taste and aroma. Take a moment to appreciate the notes of chocolate, caramel, and bright citrus that are characteristic of this esteemed coffee variety.
8. Serve your Jamaican Blue Mountain Coffee black or with your preferred additions, such as a splash of cream or a sprinkle of cinnamon. Enjoy!

Note: Jamaican Blue Mountain Coffee is a delicacy, so it's important to handle and store the beans with care. Keep them in an airtight container away from sunlight and moisture to preserve their flavors.

# Malaysian Ipoh White Coffee

**Ingredient List:**
- 4 ounces (120 ml) of freshly brewed strong coffee
- 2 tablespoons (30 ml) of condensed milk
- 1 tablespoon (15 ml) of evaporated milk
- 1 teaspoon (5 ml) of sugar (optional)
- Ice cubes

**Preparation time**: 10 minutes
**Portion Information:** Makes 1 serving
**Equipment Tips:**
- Coffee maker or French press for brewing coffee
- Whisk or spoon for mixing
- Glass or mug for serving

Detailed instructions for preparation and cooking:
1. Start by brewing a strong cup of coffee using your preferred method. Make sure it is hot and aromatic.
2. In a separate cup, mix the condensed milk and evaporated milk together until well combined. You can adjust the sweetness by adding sugar if desired.
3. Pour the hot brewed coffee into the milk mixture while continuously whisking or stirring. This will create a frothy and creamy consistency.
4. Fill a separate glass or mug with ice cubes, leaving enough space to accommodate the coffee mixture.
5. Slowly pour the coffee and milk mixture over the ice cubes. The cold temperature will help the coffee retain its rich flavor while providing a refreshing experience.
6. Give it a gentle stir to ensure all the ingredients are well incorporated.
7. Your Malaysian Ipoh White Coffee is now ready to be enjoyed! Savor the unique combination of smooth coffee flavor and creamy sweetness.

Note: This recipe is traditionally served chilled, but you can also serve it hot by skipping the ice cubes and heating the milk mixture before adding it to the coffee. Adjust the sweetness according to your preference.

Indulge in the artistry of Malaysian culinary delights with this exquisite Malaysian Ipoh White Coffee recipe. Experience the harmonious blend of strong coffee, creamy milk, and the perfect touch of sweetness. Elevate your coffee routine to a whole new level with this enchanting beverage that will surely tantalize your taste buds.

# Russian Coffee with Vodka

**Ingredient List:**
- 1 shot of espresso (30 ml / 1 oz)
- 1 shot of vodka (30 ml / 1 oz)

**Preparation time**: 5 minutes

**Portion Information:** Makes 1 serving

**Equipment Tips:**
- Espresso machine
- Shot glass or measuring cup

**Instructions:**
1. Begin by preparing a shot of espresso using an espresso machine. Make sure to follow the manufacturer's instructions for brewing the perfect shot.
2. Once the espresso is ready, pour it into a shot glass or measuring cup, and set it aside.
3. Take a shot glass or small glass and carefully measure 1 shot of vodka.
4. Slowly pour the vodka into the same glass as the espresso, and watch as the two liquids combine.
5. Give the mixture a gentle stir with a spoon, ensuring that the flavors blend harmoniously.
6. Take a moment to admire the rich, dark color of the Russian Coffee with Vodka, appreciating the beauty of this simple yet refined beverage.
7. Serve the Russian Coffee with Vodka immediately, savoring each sip and letting its bold flavors dance on your palate.
8. Enjoy this exquisite beverage as a delightful after-dinner treat or whenever you crave a sophisticated coffee experience with a hint of vodka.

# Swiss Mocha

**Ingredient List:**
- 2 ounces (60 grams) of high-quality Swiss chocolate, finely chopped
- 1 cup (240 milliliters) of freshly brewed coffee
- 1 cup (240 milliliters) of milk
- 2 tablespoons (30 grams) of granulated sugar
- 1/2 teaspoon (2.5 milliliters) of vanilla extract
- Whipped cream, for topping (optional)
- Cocoa powder, for garnish (optional)

**Preparation time**: 15 minutes
**Portion Information**: This recipe makes 2 servings.
**Equipment Tips:** To prepare Swiss Mocha, you will need the following kitchen tools: a saucepan, a whisk, a serving pitcher, coffee mugs, and optionally, a hand mixer.

**Instructions:**
1. Place the finely chopped Swiss chocolate into a saucepan set over low heat. Allow it to melt slowly, stirring occasionally with a whisk.
2. In the meantime, brew your favorite coffee using either an espresso machine or a French press.
3. Once the chocolate has melted completely, pour in the freshly brewed coffee. Stir well to combine, ensuring the chocolate is fully incorporated into the coffee.
4. In a separate saucepan, heat the milk over medium-low heat until it is warm but not boiling. Be sure to stir continuously to prevent the milk from scorching.
5. Gradually add the warm milk to the chocolate and coffee mixture, continuously whisking to create a velvety texture.
6. Stir in the granulated sugar and vanilla extract, combining all the flavors harmoniously.
7. Continue to heat the Swiss Mocha gently until it reaches your desired temperature. Avoid boiling the mixture.
8. Once the Swiss Mocha is hot enough, carefully pour it into two serving mugs.
9. If desired, top each mug with a generous dollop of whipped cream and lightly dust with cocoa powder for an extra touch of elegance.
10. Serve immediately and relish the rich, velvety flavors of Swiss Mocha.

Enjoy this exquisite Swiss Mocha as a delightful treat, perfect for cozy evenings or as an indulgent pick-me-up during the day. Happy sipping!

# Filipino Barako Coffee

**Ingredient List:**
- Filipino Barako Coffee beans - 2 ounces (56 grams)
- Hot water - 16 ounces (473 ml)
- Sweetened condensed milk - to taste

**Preparation time**: 15 minutes

**Portion Information**: Portions for 2

**Equipment Tips:**
- Coffee grinder
- French press or coffee maker
- Kettle or saucepan

**Instructions:**
1. Begin by measuring 2 ounces (56 grams) of Filipino Barako Coffee beans. This specific coffee variety is known for its strong and rich flavor, so feel free to adjust the quantity to suit your taste preferences.
2. Grind the coffee beans to a medium-coarse consistency. This can be achieved using a coffee grinder designed for this purpose. The slightly coarse grind helps in extracting the full flavor of the Barako Coffee.
3. Heat 16 ounces (473 ml) of water in a kettle or saucepan until it reaches a temperature of around 200°F (93°C). Boiling water may scorch the coffee and hinder the optimal extraction of flavors, so it's important to let it cool slightly before using.
4. While the water is heating, prepare your French press or coffee maker. Ensure it is clean and free from any residue that may affect the taste of the coffee.
5. Place the ground Barako Coffee into the French press or coffee maker's container.
6. Once the water has reached the desired temperature, carefully pour it over the coffee grounds. Make sure to evenly saturate all the coffee particles for a consistent extraction.
7. Let the coffee steep for 4 minutes. This allows the flavors to fully develop and enhances the taste.
8. In the meantime, warm your coffee cups to ensure the temperature of the brew will remain enjoyable.
9. After 4 minutes, slowly press down the plunger in the French press or let the coffee maker complete its brewing process. This separates the brewed coffee from the grounds, preventing further extraction and potential bitterness.
10. Pour the freshly brewed Barako Coffee into the warmed cups, leaving some space for customization.
11. Taste the coffee and determine whether you would like to add sweetened condensed milk. This ingredient is a popular addition in Filipino coffee culture and adds a delightful touch of sweetness. Add the desired amount to each cup, adjusting to your taste.
12. Stir the coffee and condensed milk gently, ensuring they blend harmoniously.
13. Filipino Barako Coffee is best enjoyed hot, so serve immediately and savor each sip of this robust and flavorful Filipino brew.

# Hawaiian Macadamia Nut Coffee

**Ingredient List:**
- 1 cup (240 ml) strong brewed coffee
- 1 tablespoon (15 ml) macadamia nut flavored syrup
- 2 tablespoons (30 ml) coconut milk
- Whipped cream, for topping
- Crushed macadamia nuts, for garnish

**Preparation time**: 5 minutes
**Portion Information**: This recipe makes 1 serving.

**Equipment Tips:**
- Coffee maker or French press
- Coffee mug
- Measuring spoons
- Whisk or spoon for stirring
- Small saucepan (if not using pre-made coffee)
- Blender or grinder (optional, for crushing macadamia nuts)

**Instructions:**
1. Start by brewing a strong cup of coffee using your coffee maker or French press. If you don't have pre-made coffee, heat 1 cup (240 ml) of water in a small saucepan until hot but not boiling. Add 1 tablespoon (15 ml) of finely ground coffee and let it steep for 4-5 minutes. Strain the coffee into your mug.
2. Once you have your hot coffee ready, add 1 tablespoon (15 ml) of macadamia nut flavored syrup to the mug. This will give your coffee a delightful nutty aroma and flavor.
3. Next, pour in 2 tablespoons (30 ml) of creamy coconut milk. The rich and slightly sweet coconut milk complements the macadamia flavor perfectly.
4. Stir the coffee mixture gently with a whisk or spoon until well combined.
5. If desired, top your Hawaiian Macadamia Nut Coffee with a dollop of whipped cream. This adds an extra creamy and decadent touch to your beverage.
6. For a finishing touch, garnish your coffee with a sprinkle of crushed macadamia nuts. You can crush the nuts using a blender or grinder, or simply put them in a small bag and lightly crush them with a rolling pin.
7. Serve your Hawaiian Macadamia Nut Coffee immediately and enjoy the delightful flavors of the islands in every sip.

Embrace the artistry of this coffee creation, celebrating the tropical essence of Hawaii with the nutty richness of macadamia and the creamy indulgence of coconut milk. This captivating blend of flavors will transport you to paradise with each sip. Experience the balance between the robustness of the coffee and the delightful sweetness of the macadamia nut syrup. Let the whipped cream adorn your taste buds and the crushed macadamia nuts garnish your senses. Prepare this masterpiece and elevate your coffee experience to new heights.

# Austrian Wiener Melange

**Ingredient List:**
- 1 shot of strong espresso (30 ml/1 fl. oz)
- 1 tablespoon of powdered sugar (10 gr)
- 1 cup of milk (240 ml)
- 1 teaspoon of vanilla extract (5 ml)
- Whipped cream for garnish

**Preparation time**: 10 minutes

**Portion Information**: makes 1 serving.

**Equipment Tips:**
- To prepare this delightful Austrian beverage, it is best to have the following kitchen tools:
- Espresso machine or a Moka pot
- Small saucepan
- Whisk or milk frother
- Coffee mug or glass

**Instructions:**
1. Start by brewing a strong shot of espresso using an espresso machine or a Moka pot, capturing the rich and bold flavors of the coffee.
2. In a small saucepan, heat the milk over medium-low heat until it begins to steam, but avoid boiling it. The gentle heating process will ensure the milk becomes velvety and smooth.
3. While the milk is heating, take a coffee mug or glass and add the powdered sugar. This delicate touch of sweetness will complement the bitterness of the espresso.
4. Once the milk is steaming, remove it from the heat and pour it slowly into the coffee mug, allowing the powdered sugar to dissolve completely. Use a whisk or milk frother to create a frothy texture, adding a layer of sophistication to your Wiener Melange.
5. Now, carefully pour the shot of espresso into the milk and sugar mixture. The combination of strong coffee and creamy milk will create a harmonious balance of flavors.
6. To enhance the aroma and add a delightful touch, stir in the vanilla extract. This subtle addition will elevate your Wiener Melange to new levels of decadence.
7. Lastly, complete your Austrian masterpiece by topping it with a generous dollop of whipped cream. The creamy foam will add a luxurious finishing touch to your creation, making it truly irresistible.
8. Serve your Austrian Wiener Melange immediately, allowing the enchanting flavors and magnificent presentation to dazzle your senses. Savor each sip of this delightful concoction, sipping it slowly to fully appreciate the artistry behind this classic Austrian drink.

Indulge in the magic of Austrian cuisine with this delightful Wiener Melange - a symphony of coffee, milk, and sweet flavors that will transport you to the charming streets and cozy cafes of Vienna. Enjoy the beauty in simplicity and the exquisite taste of this beloved Austrian gem.

# American Pumpkin Spice Latte

**Ingredient List:**
- 2 ounces (60 ml) of espresso or strong brewed coffee
- 1 cup (240 ml) of milk
- 1 tablespoon (15 ml) of pumpkin puree
- 1 tablespoon (15 ml) of sugar
- 1/2 teaspoon (2.5 ml) of pumpkin spice blend
- Whipped cream for topping
- Cinnamon powder for garnish

**Preparation time**: 15 minutes
**Portion Information**: Makes 1 serving
**Equipment Tips:** For best results, use an espresso machine to make the espresso. If you don't have one, a stovetop espresso maker or a French press can be used as an alternative.

Detailed instructions for preparation and cooking:
1. In a small saucepan, heat the milk over medium heat until hot but not boiling. Stir occasionally to prevent scorching.
2. In the meantime, brew your espresso or strong coffee. If using an espresso machine, follow the manufacturer's instructions. If using a stovetop espresso maker, fill the bottom chamber with water, add the coffee grounds to the filter basket, assemble the pot, and place it on the stove over medium heat. Allow the coffee to espress until all the water has passed through the grounds. If using a French press, add coffee grounds to the press, pour in hot water, let it steep for a few minutes, and then press the plunger down slowly.
3. In a microwave-safe mug, combine the pumpkin puree, sugar, and pumpkin spice blend. Microwave for about 30 seconds, or until the pumpkin is warm and the sugar has dissolved. Stir well to combine.
4. Pour the hot espresso or coffee into the mug with the pumpkin mixture. Stir until well incorporated.
5. Froth the hot milk using an electric milk frother, if available, or by vigorously shaking it in a jar with a tight lid. If frothing isn't desired, simply warm the milk to your preferred temperature.
6. Slowly pour the frothy milk into the mug, using a spoon to hold back the foam. Continue pouring until the mug is almost full, leaving some room for the foam.
7. Top the latte with a dollop of whipped cream and sprinkle some cinnamon powder over it for an extra touch of flavor.
8. Serve immediately and enjoy sipping on your delightful American Pumpkin Spice Latte

# Israeli Coffee Hafuch

**Ingredient List:**
- Strong brewed coffee - 10-12 oz (300-350 ml)
- Milk - 4-6 oz (120-180 ml)
- Granulated sugar - 1-2 tsp (5-10 gr)
- Ground cinnamon - a pinch
- Cocoa powder - for garnish

**Preparation time**: 10 minutes
**Portion Information**: Makes 1 serving
**Equipment Tips:**
- Espresso machine or stovetop coffee maker
- Milk frother or a small whisk
- Coffee cup or glass

**Instructions:**
1. Begin by brewing a strong cup of coffee using your preferred brewing method. If using an espresso machine, extract a double shot (2 oz/60 ml) of espresso.
2. While the coffee is brewing, pour the milk into a small saucepan and heat it over medium-low heat until it reaches a gentle simmer. Avoid boiling the milk as it may scorch.
3. Using a milk frother or a small whisk, froth the heated milk until it becomes creamy and thick. The temperature should be around 150°F (65°C) for the perfect hafuch.
4. Once the coffee is ready, stir in the desired amount of sugar while it is still hot, ensuring it dissolves completely.
5. Pour the hot coffee into a coffee cup or glass, leaving some space at the top for the milk foam.
6. Holding back the frothed milk with a spoon, pour the hot milk into the cup, letting it mix gently with the coffee. Gradually release the foam on top until it covers the entire surface.
7. Sprinkle a pinch of ground cinnamon over the milk foam while it's still velvety and inviting.
8. Optionally, dust the foam with a small amount of cocoa powder for added aesthetics and flavor.
9. Serve the Israeli Coffee Hafuch immediately while it is still warm and enjoy its rich flavors and smooth texture.

Note: The Israeli Coffee Hafuch is typically enjoyed without stirring to relish the distinct layers of coffee, milk, and foam. However, feel free to stir gently if desired before drinking.

# Nigerian Coffee

**Ingredient List:**
- 1 cup (240 ml) of strong black coffee
- 2 tablespoons (30 ml) of condensed milk
- 1 tablespoon (15 ml) of evaporated milk
- 1 teaspoon (5 ml) of cocoa powder
- 1/4 teaspoon (1.25 ml) of ground cinnamon
- 1/4 teaspoon (1.25 ml) of nutmeg
- Whipped cream, for garnish (optional)

**Preparation time**: 10 minutes
**Portion Information**: This recipe serves 1 person.
**Equipment Tips:** To enjoy the full flavors and aromas of this coffee, it is recommended to use a French press or a coffee maker. Alternatively, you can use a regular coffee pot or a coffee filter cone.

**Instructions:**
1. Start by brewing a strong black coffee using your preferred method. Make sure the coffee is hot and freshly brewed for the optimal taste experience.
2. In a small saucepan, pour the condensed milk and evaporated milk. Place the saucepan over low heat, stirring continuously until the two milks combine and become smooth. Be careful not to let it boil.
3. Add the cocoa powder, ground cinnamon, and nutmeg to the milk mixture. Continue stirring until the cocoa powder is fully dissolved and the spices are well incorporated. The aromatic blend of spices will complement the robust taste of the coffee.
4. Pour the brewed black coffee into a large mug, leaving some space at the top for the milk mixture. Slowly pour the spiced milk into the coffee, gradually stirring to ensure even distribution of flavors.
5. For an indulgent touch, top your Nigerian Nigerian Coffee with a dollop of whipped cream. You can also sprinkle a pinch of cocoa powder or grated chocolate on top for an added visual appeal.
6. Serve while hot and savor the unique flavors of this Nigerian delight. As you take your first sip, prepare to be transported to the rich and vibrant culinary world of Nigeria.

Note: Feel free to adjust the sweetness and spiciness of this coffee to your liking. You can increase or decrease the amount of condensed milk, spices, or even add a dash of vanilla extract for a personal touch. Enjoy this delightful cup of Nigerian Nigerian Coffee alone or with a traditional Nigerian snack for a truly immersive experience.

# Vietnamese Coffee

**Ingredient List:**
- 2 large eggs (120 gr)
- 4 tablespoons condensed milk (60 ml)
- 4 tablespoons Vietnamese coffee powder (60 gr)
- 1 cup hot water (240 ml)
- Ice cubes (optional)

**Preparation time**: 15 minutes

**Portion Information:** This recipe makes 2 servings.

**Equipment Tips:**
- Make sure to have a small heat-resistant glass or cup with a handle for serving.
- A French press or a Vietnamese coffee filter is best for brewing the coffee.

**Instructions:**
1. Crack the eggs and separate the egg yolks from the whites. Place the egg yolks in a mixing bowl and set aside the egg whites for another use.
2. Add the condensed milk to the egg yolks and whisk together until well combined. This mixture will serve as the creamy topping for the coffee.
3. Brew the Vietnamese coffee powder in a French press or using a Vietnamese coffee filter. If using a French press, add the coffee powder and hot water to the press, stir, cover with a plunger, and let it steep for 4 minutes. Press the plunger down slowly to separate the coffee grounds from the liquid. If using a Vietnamese coffee filter, follow the manufacturer's instructions.
4. Once the coffee is brewed, divide it equally between two cups.
5. Carefully spoon the creamy egg mixture on top of each cup of coffee. The creamy layer should be dense and luscious.
6. Using a small whisk or spoon, gently stir the creamy egg mixture into the coffee until well incorporated. The mixture should create a creamy texture, adding depth and richness to the coffee.
7. Serve the Vietnamese Egg Coffee hot or pour it over ice cubes for a refreshing twist.

Enjoy this intriguing culinary creation that beautifully combines the flavors of coffee and eggs. The creamy, velvety texture of the egg mixture harmonizes perfectly with the strong Vietnamese coffee, creating a unique and delightful drinking experience. Savor this artistic masterpiece, which exemplifies the true essence of Vietnamese cuisine.

# Egyptian Sada Coffee

**Ingredient List:**
- Ground Arabic coffee beans - 2 tablespoons (30 grams)
- Cold water - 2 cups (480 milliliters)
- Sugar - to taste
- Cardamom pods - 2, crushed

**Preparation time**: 15 minutes

**Portion Information**: Makes 2 cups

**Equipment Tips:**
- Traditional Arabic coffee pot (dallah) or a small saucepan
- Coffee grinder or mortar and pestle
- Heat source (stove or electric burner)
- Ceramic cups for serving

**Instructions:**
1. Start by grinding the Arabic coffee beans to a medium-fine consistency using a coffee grinder or mortar and pestle. The aroma should be intoxicating, filling your kitchen with the scent of rich coffee beans.
2. In a traditional Arabic coffee pot (dallah) or a small saucepan, combine the freshly ground coffee, cold water, crushed cardamom pods, and sugar to taste. Remember, the sweetness level is based on personal preference, so adjust accordingly.
3. Place the pot or saucepan on a heat source, whether it's a stove or an electric burner. Slowly bring the mixture to a boil over medium heat, stirring occasionally to ensure the flavors meld together harmoniously.
4. As the coffee starts to bubble and rise, watch it closely to prevent any overflow. Usually, this takes about 5-7 minutes.
5. Once the coffee has reached its boiling point, reduce the heat to low and let it simmer gently for another 5 minutes. This step is crucial as it allows the flavors to intensify and develop further.
6. After the simmering process, remove the pot or saucepan from the heat source. Allow the coffee to settle for a few moments, allowing the fine coffee grounds to sink to the bottom.
7. To serve, carefully pour the brewed Egyptian Sada Coffee into ceramic cups, ensuring that the settled coffee grounds remain undisturbed in the pot or saucepan.
8. Egyptians traditionally serve the Sada Coffee in small cups and enjoy it alongside a glass of cold water or a small dessert for a perfect balance of flavors.

Enjoy this authentic Egyptian Sada Coffee, a ritualistic beverage that signifies warmth, hospitality, and the art of true culinary craftsmanship.

# Puerto Rican Café con Leche

**Ingredient List:**
- 2 ounces (60 ml) of strong brewed coffee
- 4 ounces (120 ml) of milk
- 1 teaspoon (5 grams) of sugar (optional)

**Preparation time**: 5 minutes
**Portion Information**: Makes 1 serving
**Equipment Tips:**
- A small saucepan
- A whisk or a small hand-held blender

**Instructions:**
1. Start by brewing a strong cup of coffee using your preferred method. Use 2 ounces (60 ml) of the brewed coffee for this recipe. Set it aside momentarily.
2. In a small saucepan, pour the milk and heat it over medium-low heat. As the milk warms up, stir occasionally to prevent it from scorching on the bottom of the pan. It should not come to a boil but reach a hot temperature.
3. Once the milk is heated, use a whisk or a small hand-held blender to froth the milk. If you prefer a creamier consistency, continue whisking or blending until a thick foam forms on top.
4. Pour the brewed coffee into a large coffee cup or mug.
5. Now, you have two options for combining the coffee and milk. For a classic café con leche style, pour the frothed milk over the coffee. This method creates a beautiful layered effect as the milk sinks to the bottom, creating a visually appealing drink.
6. If you prefer a more evenly mixed café con leche, pour the heated milk into the coffee while stirring gently. This way, the milk and coffee blend together to form a delicious creamy beverage.
7. If desired, add a teaspoon of sugar to sweeten the café con leche. However, keep in mind that traditionally Puerto Rican café con leche is not excessively sweet, allowing the natural flavors to shine through.
8. Give your café con leche a final stir, ensuring all the ingredients are well combined.
9. Serve the Puerto Rican Café con Leche immediately while hot, savoring each sip of its rich and delicate flavor.

Enjoy the perfect harmony of strong coffee and creamy milk in this delightful Puerto Rican Café con Leche!

# Indonesian Kopi Tubruk

**Ingredient List:**
- 2 tablespoons (30 ml) finely ground coffee beans
- 6 ounces (180 ml) hot water
- Sugar (optional), according to taste

**Preparation time**: 5 minutes

**Portion Information**: 1 serving

**Equipment Tips:** For the best results, use a small coffee pot with a long spout, called a "cezve" or "jebena," or a French press can work as well.

**Instructions:**
1. Begin by heating the water. You can either bring the water to a boil using a kettle or heat it on the stove until it's hot but not boiling.
2. While the water is heating, add the finely ground coffee to the cup or coffee pot. Finely ground coffee will ensure a rich and robust flavor.
3. Once the water is hot, slowly pour it over the coffee grounds. Make sure to pour it in a circular motion, allowing the water to evenly saturate the coffee.
4. Let the coffee brew and steep for 1-2 minutes. This will allow the flavors to develop fully.
5. If desired, you can add sugar to taste. Traditionally, Kopi Tubruk is served without milk, but feel free to add a splash of milk if you prefer a creamier taste.
6. After stirring the coffee and sugar (if using), let it sit for another minute to settle.
7. Finally, pour your aromatic Kopi Tubruk into a cup, making sure to pour it carefully to avoid any coffee grounds in your cup. Take a moment to appreciate the captivating aroma and the beautiful reddish-brown color of the brew.
8. Savor each sip slowly. Indonesian Kopi Tubruk embodies the true essence of the coffee experience, with its robust flavors and natural simplicity.

Enjoy this delightful and authentic Indonesian coffee experience!

# Indonesian Pandan Coffee

**Ingredient List:**
- 1 ½ cups (355 ml) of water
- 2 tablespoons (14 grams) of ground coffee beans
- 2-3 pandan leaves, washed and tied in a knot
- 1 teaspoon (5 ml) of condensed milk
- Ice cubes
- Sugar (optional, to taste)

**Preparation time**: 10 minutes

**Portion Information:** Serves 1

**Equipment Tips:**
- Saucepan or kettle for boiling water
- Coffee filter or French press for brewing coffee
- Tall glass or mason jar for serving
- Stirring spoon or straw for mixing
- Blender (optional, for a frothy version)

**Instructions:**
1. Boil the water: In a saucepan or kettle, bring the water to a boil.
2. Brew the coffee: While the water is boiling, place the ground coffee beans into a coffee filter or French press. Pour the hot water over the coffee and let it steep for about 4 minutes. If using a French press, gently press the plunger down after 4 minutes to separate the grounds from the liquid.
3. Add pandan leaves: Once the coffee is brewed, add the tied pandan leaves to the coffee while it's still hot. This will infuse the aromatic pandan flavor into the coffee. Let it steep for an additional 5 minutes.
4. Sweeten it up: Remove the pandan leaves from the coffee. Stir in condensed milk to add a touch of creaminess and sweetness. Adjust the sweetness by adding sugar, if desired.
5. Chill and serve: Pour the pandan coffee into a glass filled with ice cubes. Stir well to incorporate the flavors. Optionally, for a frothy version, transfer the coffee and a few ice cubes to a blender and blend until frothy.
6. Enjoy: Sip and savor the delightful Indonesian Pandan Coffee! The unique blend of pandan's floral notes with the richness of coffee will transport you to the enchanting streets of Indonesia.

Note: Pandan leaves are naturally fragrant and can be found in most Asian grocery stores. If they are not available, you can use pandan extract or essence as a substitute. Adjust the amount according to taste.

# Japanese Kyoto-style Cold Brew

**Ingredient List:**
- 50g (1.76oz) Japanese Kyoto-style coffee beans
- 500ml (16.9 fl oz) cold, filtered water

**Preparation time**: 12 hours
**Portion Information**: 1 portion
**Equipment Tips:**

- Siphon coffee maker (optional)
- Coffee grinder (preferably a burr grinder)
- Glass carafe or pitcher
- Fine-mesh sieve or cheesecloth
- Ice cubes (for serving)

**Instructions:**
1. Start by selecting the finest quality Japanese Kyoto-style coffee beans available to ensure a delightful and authentic flavor experience.
2. Weigh out 50g (1.76oz) of the coffee beans, as precision is key to achieving the perfect balance of flavors.
3. For the utmost freshness and flavor, grind the coffee beans just before brewing. If using a siphon coffee maker, grind the beans to a medium-fine consistency. If using a regular coffee maker or French press, aim for a coarse grind.
4. Place the ground coffee in the siphon coffee maker's upper chamber or directly into a glass carafe or pitcher for other brewing methods.
5. Measure 500ml (16.9 fl oz) of cold, filtered water. Add the water to the coffee grounds, ensuring all the grounds are saturated and fully immersed.
6. Gently stir the mixture to facilitate an even extraction. This will contribute to the complex and well-rounded flavor profile we seek to achieve.
7. Allow the coffee to steep for a minimum of 12 hours. This extended period captures the delicate nuances and characteristics of the Kyoto-style brewing process.
8. Once the steeping time has passed, carefully separate the coffee grounds from the extracted liquid. For a smooth and sediment-free result, you can use a fine-mesh sieve or, even better, a cheesecloth.

9. After straining, transfer the cold brew into a glass carafe or pitcher, creating a visual invitation to indulge in this artful creation.
10. If desired, serve the Japanese Kyoto-style Cold Brew over ice for a refreshing and invigorating experience. The addition of ice cubes enhances the presentation and adds an element of elegance.
11. Savor each sip, allowing the meticulously extracted flavors to dance upon your palate. Experience the harmony of Japanese Kyoto-style Cold Brew in its purest form, unraveled through a unique brewing process.

Note: The Japanese Kyoto-style Cold Brew can be stored in the refrigerator for up to 3 days, delighting in its extraordinary flavor every time you pour a glass.

Embrace the artistry of Japanese Kyoto-style Cold Brew and enjoy the tranquil indulgence it brings to your senses.

## Belgian Speculoos Latte

**Ingredient List:**
- 1.7 oz (50 gr) Speculoos cookie crumbs
- 1.1 oz (30 ml) Speculoos syrup
- 8.5 oz (250 ml) milk (preferably whole milk)
- 0.5 oz (15 gr) dark chocolate
- 2 shots of espresso
- Whipped cream for topping
- Cinnamon powder for garnish

**Preparation Time**: 10 minutes
**Portion Information**: 1 serving
**Equipment Tips:** You will need an espresso machine, a milk frother, and a blender or food processor to crush the Speculoos cookies.

**Instructions:**
1. Begin by preparing your espresso shots using the espresso machine. Set them aside for later use.

2. Take the Speculoos cookies and, using a blender or food processor, crush them into fine crumbs. Ensure there are no large pieces remaining. Set aside a teaspoon of the crumbled cookies for garnish.
3. In a small saucepan, heat the milk over medium heat until it simmers. Be careful not to let it boil. Once the milk is simmering, remove it from the heat.
4. Add the Speculoos syrup and half of the crushed Speculoos cookie crumbs (approximately 0.85 oz or 25 gr) to the saucepan with the hot milk. Stir well until the syrup and cookies are fully incorporated in the milk, forming a rich, spiced mixture.
5. Place the dark chocolate in a heatproof bowl and melt it in the microwave or over a double boiler, stirring occasionally until smooth.
6. Pour the melted dark chocolate into a coffee mug, coating the sides with the chocolate as you pour. This step adds a delightful touch of decadence to your latte.
7. Now, it's time to assemble your Belgian Speculoos Latte. Start by pouring the espresso shots into the chocolate-coated mug.
8. Next, gently pour the warm Speculoos milk mixture into the mug, filling it almost to the top. Leave a little space for the whipped cream.
9. Froth the remaining milk using a milk frother until it reaches a creamy and velvety consistency.
10. Carefully spoon a generous amount of frothed milk on top of the latte, creating a beautiful foam layer.
11. Garnish your Belgian Speculoos Latte with a dollop of whipped cream, a sprinkle of cinnamon powder, and the remaining teaspoon of crushed Speculoos cookies.
12. Serve the latte immediately and savor the aromatic combination of coffee, spices, and creamy indulgence. Enjoy this exquisite beverage as a delightful treat during breakfast or a cozy afternoon pick-me-up.

Note: You can customize your latte by adjusting the sweetness with more or less Speculoos syrup, and varying the amount of cookie crumbs for a stronger or milder flavor.

# Brazilian Cinnamon Coffee

**Ingredient List:**
- Ground coffee - 3 tablespoons (20g)
- Water - 2 cups (480ml)
- Cinnamon stick - 1
- Sweetened condensed milk - 3 tablespoons (60g)

**Preparation time**: 10 minutes

**Portion Information:** Makes 2 servings

**Equipment Tips:**
- Coffee grinder (if using whole beans)
- Coffee maker or French press
- Saucepan
- Stirring spoon
- Coffee mugs

**Instructions:**
1. Start by grinding your coffee beans if you're using whole beans. Aim for a medium grind size.
2. In a saucepan, combine the water and ground coffee. Add the cinnamon stick to the mixture.
3. Place the saucepan over medium heat and bring the coffee to a gentle boil. Stir occasionally to prevent the grounds from settling at the bottom.
4. Once the coffee reaches a boil, reduce the heat to low and let it simmer for about 5 minutes. This simmering will enhance the flavors and aromas by infusing the cinnamon stick.
5. After 5 minutes, remove the saucepan from the heat and allow it to cool for a minute or two.
6. Carefully strain the coffee using a fine-mesh sieve to separate the grounds and cinnamon stick. You can also use a coffee filter if desired.
7. Now it's time to sweeten your Brazilian Cinnamon Coffee. Add 3 tablespoons of sweetened condensed milk to the strained coffee. Stir well until the milk is fully incorporated.
8. Pour the beautifully fragrant coffee into coffee mugs, dividing it evenly between each mug.
9. Serve your Brazilian Cinnamon Coffee while it's still hot and enjoy the delightful flavors and warmth of this traditional Brazilian beverage.

Note: You can garnish your coffee with a sprinkle of ground cinnamon or a cinnamon stick for an extra touch of elegance. Cheers to the amazing taste of Brazil!

# Mexican Spicy Mocha

**Ingredient List:**
- 1 espresso shot (30 ml, 1 fl oz)
- 1 tablespoon cocoa powder (7 gr)
- 1/2 teaspoon ground cinnamon (1 gr)
- 1/4 teaspoon ground cayenne pepper (0.5 gr)
- 1 cup milk (240 ml, 8 fl oz)
- 1 tablespoon sugar (12 gr)
- Whipped cream, for topping
- Ground cinnamon, for garnish

**Preparation time**: 10 minutes
**Portion Information**: Makes 1 serving
**Equipment Tips:** It is recommended to use an espresso machine to make the espresso shot. A milk frother or small saucepan can be used to heat and froth the milk.

**Instructions:**
1. Brew a fresh espresso shot using your espresso machine. If you don't have an espresso machine, you can use a strongly brewed cup of coffee as a substitute.
2. In a small bowl, whisk together the cocoa powder, ground cinnamon, and ground cayenne pepper. This combination of spices will add a delightful kick to your mocha.
3. In a saucepan or using a milk frother, heat the milk over medium heat until hot but not boiling. Make sure to continuously stir the milk to prevent it from scorching.
4. Add the sugar to the heated milk and continue stirring until it has completely dissolved.
5. Slowly sprinkle the cocoa powder and spice mixture into the hot milk, whisking vigorously. This will ensure that the flavors are evenly incorporated.
6. Pour the prepared espresso shot into a large mug. Then, slowly pour the spiced milk mixture over the espresso. Gently stir to combine the flavors.
7. To enhance the presentation, top your Mexican Spicy Mocha with a dollop of whipped cream. You can also sprinkle a dash of ground cinnamon on top for an extra touch of warmth and aroma.

Enjoy your Mexican Spicy Mocha while it's still hot and savor the rich flavors of chocolate, cinnamon, and a hint of spicy cayenne. This indulgent beverage is perfect for cozy mornings or as an afternoon pick-me-up. Embrace the culinary artistry of this unique twist on a classic mocha and let your taste buds dance with delight.

# Lebanese Cardamom Coffee

**Ingredient List:**
- 4.5 grams (0.16 ounces) of ground Arabic coffee beans
- 2 cardamom pods
- 250 milliliters (8.45 fluid ounces) of water
- Sugar, to taste

**Preparation time**: 10 minutes

**Portion Information**: serves 1 person.

**Equipment Tips:**
To make the perfect Lebanese Cardamom Coffee, you will need the following:
- Coffee grinder
- Small pot or cezve
- Stove

**Instructions:**
1. Start by grinding the Arabic coffee beans to a medium-fine consistency. The aroma will awaken your senses, paving the way for the delightful flavors of this Lebanese delicacy.
2. Take the cardamom pods and gently crack them open. This will release their fragrant seeds, which will infuse the coffee with their distinct aroma and taste.
3. In a small pot or cezve, add the water and the cracked cardamom pods. Bring the water to a gentle boil, allowing the lovely flavors of the cardamom to steep into the liquid.
4. Once the water has come to a boil, reduce the heat to low and add the ground Arabic coffee to the pot. Let it simmer gently for about 1 minute, allowing the coffee to release its full-bodied flavor.
5. At this point, you may want to add sugar to your preference. Lebanese Cardamom Coffee is typically enjoyed with a touch of sweetness. Feel free to adjust the amount of sugar according to your taste.
6. Allow the coffee to simmer for an additional 2-3 minutes. During this time, the coffee and cardamom will meld together, creating a harmonious symphony of flavors and aromas.
7. Once the coffee is ready, remove it from the heat and let it sit undisturbed for a minute or two. This will allow the coffee grounds to settle at the bottom of the pot, ensuring a smooth and sediment-free cup of coffee.
8. Now, it's time to pour. Gently ladle the Lebanese Cardamom Coffee into small cups or demitasse espresso cups, being cautious not to disturb the sediment at the bottom.
9. As you lift the cup, notice how the rich aroma wafts up, enticing you to take that first sip. Take a moment to savor the fragrance before indulging in this exquisite Lebanese treat.
10. Lebanese Cardamom Coffee is best enjoyed alongside good company, engaging conversation, and perhaps a small sweet treat. Allow the coffee to warm your soul as you immerse yourself in the artistry of Lebanese culinary traditions.

# Chinese Red Bean Coffee

**Ingredient List:**
- Chinese red beans - 2 ounces (56 grams)
- Water - 4 cups (946 ml)
- Sweetened condensed milk - 1 cup (236 ml)
- Sugar - 2 tablespoons (28 grams)
- Coffee powder - 2 tablespoons (14 grams)
- Ground cinnamon - 1/2 teaspoon (1 gram)
- Whipped cream - for garnish (optional)

**Preparation time**: 8 hours (including overnight soaking)
**Portion Information**: Makes 4 servings
**Equipment Tips:**
- Medium-sized pot with a lid
- Blender or immersion blender
- Fine-mesh strainer or cheesecloth
- Coffee maker or French press (optional)
- Coffee grinder (if using whole coffee beans)
- Coffee mug or cup for serving
- Whisk or spoon for stirring

**Instructions:**
1. Rinse the Chinese red beans under cold water to remove any impurities and drain.
2. Place the rinsed red beans in a medium-sized pot and add 4 cups of water. Bring to a boil over high heat.
3. Once boiling, reduce the heat to low and let the beans simmer for about 2 minutes. Then, turn off the heat, cover with a lid, and let the beans soak for at least 8 hours or overnight.
4. After the soaking time, drain the soaked red beans and rinse them with cold water again.
5. In the same pot, add the soaked red beans, 4 cups of fresh water, sweetened condensed milk, sugar, coffee powder, and ground cinnamon.
6. Place the pot over medium heat and bring the mixture to a simmer, stirring occasionally to dissolve the sugar and coffee powder.
7. Once simmering, reduce the heat to low and let the mixture cook for about 20 minutes, stirring occasionally to prevent sticking.
8. After 20 minutes, remove the pot from the heat and let the mixture cool slightly.
9. Using a blender or immersion blender, blend the mixture until smooth and creamy. Alternatively, you can strain the mixture using a fine-mesh strainer or cheesecloth for a smoother texture.

10. If desired, use a coffee maker or French press to brew strong coffee separately. Then, add the brewed coffee to the red bean mixture for an extra kick of caffeine.
11. Pour the Chinese Red Bean Coffee into coffee mugs or cups for serving.
12. Optionally, top each serving with a dollop of whipped cream and a sprinkle of ground cinnamon.
13. Serve the Chinese Red Bean Coffee warm and enjoy the unique and aromatic flavors.

Note: Chinese Red Bean Coffee can be served both hot and iced. Simply let the mixture cool completely after blending and then refrigerate until chilled. Serve over ice for a refreshing iced coffee variation. Enjoy!

## Guatemalan Atol de Elote Coffee

**Ingredient List:**

- 2 ears of fresh corn (480 gr)
- 2 cups of water (480 ml)
- 2 cups of milk (480 ml)
- 1 cinnamon stick
- 1/4 cup of sugar (50 gr)
- 1/4 teaspoon of vanilla extract (1.25 ml)
- 1/4 teaspoon of ground nutmeg (1.25 gr)
- 2 teaspoons of instant coffee (10 gr)

**Preparation time**: 30 minutes

**Portion Information**: This recipe makes 4 servings.

**Equipment Tips:** You will need a saucepan, blender, and a fine-mesh strainer for best results.

**Instructions:**

1. Start by husking the fresh corn and removing the silk. Using a sharp knife, carefully cut the kernels off the cob. Make sure to collect all the kernels in a bowl and set them aside.

2. In a large saucepan, combine the water and corn kernels. Place the cinnamon stick in the saucepan and bring the mixture to a boil over medium heat. Allow it to simmer for about 20 minutes, or until the corn kernels are tender.
3. Once the corn kernels are cooked, remove the saucepan from the heat. Take out the cinnamon stick and discard it.
4. Transfer the mixture to a blender and blend until smooth. Be careful as the mixture will be hot. Blend in batches if necessary.
5. Place a fine-mesh strainer over a large bowl or jug, and pour the blended mixture through it. Use a spatula to help strain out any remaining solids and separate the silky smooth liquid. Discard the solids.
6. Return the strained mixture back to the saucepan and add the milk, sugar, vanilla extract, and ground nutmeg. Stir well to combine all the ingredients.
7. Place the saucepan back on the stove over medium heat. Slowly heat the mixture while stirring constantly until it begins to simmer.
8. In a separate small bowl, dissolve the instant coffee in a few tablespoons of hot water. Once dissolved, add the coffee mixture to the saucepan and stir well.
9. Continue simmering the mixture for an additional 5 minutes, ensuring everything is well mixed and heated through.
10. Remove the saucepan from the heat and let the Guatemalan Atol de Elote Coffee cool slightly.
11. Serve the Atol de Elote Coffee hot in individual mugs or cups. Optionally, you can sprinkle a pinch of ground nutmeg on top for added flavor and garnish.

Enjoy this traditional Guatemalan delicacy with its unique combination of sweet corn, fragrant spices, and rich coffee flavor. Share it with friends and family, and savor the artistry of the culinary experience.

# Peruvian Inca Mocha

**Ingredient List:**
- 2 ounces (60 ml) of strong brewed coffee
- 1 ounce (30 ml) of dark chocolate, finely chopped
- 1 ounce (30 ml) of condensed milk
- 1/2 teaspoon (2 grams) of ground cinnamon
- 1/4 teaspoon (1 gram) of ground cayenne pepper
- 1/2 teaspoon (2 grams) of vanilla extract
- Whipped cream, for garnish
- Cocoa powder, for dusting

**Preparation time:** 10 minutes
**Portion Information:** 1 serving.
**Equipment Tips:**
- An espresso machine or coffee maker for brewing the coffee.
- A small saucepan for melting the chocolate.
- A whisk for combining the ingredients.
- A mug for serving.

**Instructions:**
1. In a small saucepan, heat the brewed coffee over medium-low heat until hot but not boiling.
2. Add the finely chopped dark chocolate to the pan and stir until fully melted and smooth.
3. Pour in the condensed milk and whisk vigorously until well combined.
4. Sprinkle the ground cinnamon and cayenne pepper into the mixture, followed by the vanilla extract. Continue whisking to incorporate all the flavors evenly.
5. Once the mixture is smooth and well blended, remove it from the heat and pour it into a mug.
6. Top the Peruvian Inca Mocha with a generous amount of whipped cream, ensuring it covers the entire surface of the drink.
7. For an artistic touch, lightly dust the whipped cream with cocoa powder. This will add visual appeal and a touch of bitterness to complement the sweetness of the mocha.
8. Serve the Peruvian Inca Mocha immediately while still warm, and enjoy the exquisite blend of rich coffee, velvety chocolate, and warm spices.

Indulge in this captivating Peruvian Inca Mocha, a true masterpiece of culinary artistry that combines the flavors of ancient Peru with the delights of modern coffee culture.

# Colombian Caramel Macchiato

**Ingredient List:**
- Colombian coffee beans - 1.76 oz (50 gr)
- Milk - 10.14 fl oz (300 ml)
- Sugar - 1.76 oz (50 gr)
- Caramel sauce - 1 tbsp
- Whipped cream - for garnish

**Preparation time**: 10 minutes
**Portion Information**: 1 serving

**Equipment Tips:**
- Coffee grinder
- Espresso machine or coffee maker
- Frothing pitcher or saucepan for frothing milk
- Whisk or electric milk frother
- Coffee mug or glass
- Spoon

**Instructions:**
1. Start by grinding the Colombian coffee beans to a medium-fine consistency. This will ensure a balanced flavor in your macchiato.
2. Prepare your espresso shot using an espresso machine or coffee maker, following the manufacturer's instructions. Once ready, set it aside.
3. In a small saucepan or frothing pitcher, pour the milk and heat it over medium heat. While heating, whisk gently to create a velvety texture. Be careful not to let it boil.
4. Once the milk is hot and frothy, remove it from the heat and set it aside.
5. In a coffee mug or glass, drizzle the caramel sauce on the bottom and along the sides. This will add a delightful sweetness and visual appeal to your macchiato.
6. Pour the freshly prepared espresso shot over the caramel sauce, slowly to create beautiful layers.
7. Now it's time to add the frothed milk. Gently pour it into the mug, allowing it to float on top of the espresso. The frothed milk will create a distinct separation of colors, which is characteristic of a macchiato.
8. To enhance the visual presentation, you can use a spoon to gently push the frothed milk towards the center, creating an artful design.
9. Finish off your Colombian Caramel Macchiato by adding a dollop of whipped cream on top. This will add a luxurious touch and a creamy element to every sip.
10. Serve immediately and enjoy the culinary artistry of a perfectly crafted Colombian Caramel Macchiato.

# French Caramel Macchiato

**Ingredient List:**
- 2 fl oz (60 ml) espresso
- 8 fl oz (240 ml) milk
- 1.5 tbsp (22 ml) caramel syrup
- Whipped cream, to garnish
- Caramel sauce, to drizzle

**Preparation time**: 5 minutes
**Portion Information**: Makes 1 serving

**Equipment Tips:**
- Espresso machine or stovetop espresso maker
- Milk frother or small saucepan
- Coffee mug
- Whisk or spoon
- Whipped cream dispenser (optional)

**Instructions:**
1. Prepare the espresso using your espresso machine or stovetop espresso maker. Aim for a strong and concentrated shot of espresso.
2. In a separate container, heat the milk until hot but not boiling. You can use a milk frother or a small saucepan on the stovetop. The milk should be heated to approximately 150°F (65°C).
3. Pour the caramel syrup into the bottom of a coffee mug.
4. Slowly pour the hot espresso over the caramel syrup, using caution to avoid splashing.
5. Next, pour the hot milk into the mug, holding back the foam with a spoon or whisk.
6. If desired, use a handheld milk frother to create some foam with the remaining milk. Alternatively, you can heat a small amount of milk separately, froth it, and spoon it over the drink.
7. Top the French Caramel Macchiato with a dollop of whipped cream.
8. Drizzle caramel sauce over the whipped cream for an alluring finishing touch.
9. Serve the French Caramel Macchiato immediately and enjoy the delightful combination of smooth espresso, velvety milk, and decadent caramel flavors.

# South Korean Banana Latte

**Ingredient List:**
- Ripe bananas - 2 (200g, 7 oz)
- Milk - 2 cups (500ml, 16 fl oz)
- Instant coffee - 2 tablespoons (20g, 0.7 oz)
- Honey - 2 tablespoons (30 ml, 1 fl oz)
- Ground cinnamon - 1/4 teaspoon (0.5g, 0.02 oz)
- Vanilla extract - 1/2 teaspoon (2.5ml, 0.1 fl oz)
- Whipped cream - for garnish
- Cocoa powder - for dusting

**Preparation time**: 10 minutes
**Portion Information:** Makes 2 servings
**Equipment Tips:**
- Blender or immersion blender
- Large saucepan or pot
- Whisk or spoon
- Cups or mugs for serving

**Instructions:**
1. Peel the ripe bananas and cut them into small chunks.
2. In a large saucepan or pot, heat the milk over medium heat until it starts to steam. Do not let it boil.
3. Add the instant coffee, honey, ground cinnamon, and vanilla extract to the heated milk. Whisk or stir until everything is well combined.
4. Carefully pour the mixture into a blender or use an immersion blender directly in the pot. Blend on high speed until the bananas are fully incorporated and the mixture becomes smooth and frothy.
5. Return the blended mixture to the saucepan or pot and heat it gently over low heat until it reaches your desired serving temperature. Stir occasionally to prevent the bottom from scorching.
6. Once heated, remove the South Korean Banana Latte from the heat and pour it into cups or mugs.
7. Top each serving with a generous dollop of whipped cream and lightly dust with cocoa powder for an elegant touch.
8. Serve immediately and enjoy the delightful creaminess and natural sweetness of this South Korean Banana Latte.

# Japanese Espresso Tonic

**Ingredient List:**
- 2 ounces (60 ml) espresso
- 4 ounces (120 ml) tonic water
- Ice cubes
- Fresh mint leaves, for garnish

**Preparation time**: 5 minutes
**Portion Information**: 1 serving
**Equipment Tips:**

To make this Japanese Espresso Tonic, you will need:
- An espresso machine or moka pot to brew the espresso.
- A tall glass to serve the drink.
- A long spoon for stirring.
- A cocktail shaker (optional) for a more vibrant presentation.

**Instructions:**
1. Start by brewing your espresso using an espresso machine or moka pot. Aim for a rich and bold extraction to balance with the tonic water.
2. Fill a tall glass with ice cubes, allowing them to chill the glass for a moment.
3. Pour the freshly brewed espresso over the ice, allowing it to cool slightly.
4. Gently pour the tonic water into the glass, ensuring a slow and steady pour to avoid excessive bubbling.
5. Optionally, if you want to intensify the flavors and presentation, you can transfer the mixture to a cocktail shaker filled with ice and shake it gently. This will create a frothy layer on top.
6. Once you have achieved the desired blend of flavors, take a long spoon and give the Japanese Espresso Tonic a gentle stir, so the coffee and tonic water marry harmoniously.
7. Garnish your creation with a sprig of fresh mint leaves, which will add a touch of aromatic freshness and enhance the visual appeal.
8. Serve immediately while it's still cold and fresh. Sip slowly, savoring the unique combination of smooth espresso and effervescent tonic water.

# Dutch Koffie Verkeerd

**Ingredient List:**

- 1 shot of espresso (30 ml / 1 ounce)
- ¾ cup of milk (180 ml / 6.1 ounces)
- A pinch of ground cinnamon
- A pinch of cocoa powder

**Preparation time:** 10 minutes

**Portion Information**: Makes 1 serving

**Equipment Tips:**

You will need a espresso machine (or a stovetop espresso maker), a saucepan, a milk frother (or a small whisk), and a coffee cup.

**Instructions:**

1. Start by making a shot of espresso using your espresso machine or stovetop espresso maker. Make sure the espresso is strong and aromatic.
2. In a saucepan, heat the milk over medium heat until it starts to steam. Be careful not to let it boil.
3. While the milk is heating, you can use a milk frother or a small whisk to froth the milk. This will create a velvety texture that is perfect for your Koffie Verkeerd.
4. Once the milk is hot and frothy, remove it from the heat.
5. Pour the shot of espresso into a coffee cup, followed by the frothed milk. The ratio of espresso to milk should be around 1:3.
6. Gently sprinkle a pinch of ground cinnamon and cocoa powder on top of the milk foam. This will add a touch of flavor and visual appeal to your Koffie Verkeerd.
7. Serve immediately and enjoy your elegant and delicious Dutch Koffie Verkeerd!

# Ecuadorian Quaker Coffee

**Ingredient List:**
- 1 cup (240 ml) water
- 2 tablespoons (14 grams) Quaker oats
- 2 tablespoons (25 grams) brown sugar
- 2 tablespoons (30 ml) condensed milk
- 1 tablespoon (6 grams) unsweetened cocoa powder
- 1/2 teaspoon (2.5 grams) ground cinnamon
- 1/4 teaspoon (1 gram) vanilla extract
- 1 espresso shot (30 ml)
- Whipped cream (for topping)
- Cocoa powder (for dusting)

Preparation time: 15 minutes
Portion Information: 1 serving
**Equipment Tips:** A small saucepan, a coffee maker or espresso machine, a whisk, and a coffee cup.

**Instructions:**
1. In a small saucepan, bring the water to a gentle boil over medium-low heat.
2. Add the Quaker oats to the boiling water and cook for about 5 minutes, stirring occasionally until the oats are soft and tender.
3. Remove the saucepan from heat and let it cool for a minute.
4. Using a whisk, vigorously stir the brown sugar, condensed milk, unsweetened cocoa powder, ground cinnamon, and vanilla extract into the oats until well combined.
5. Return the saucepan to low heat and simmer the mixture for another 3-4 minutes, stirring continuously to ensure it doesn't stick to the bottom.
6. Meanwhile, prepare an espresso shot using a coffee maker or espresso machine.
7. Once the coffee is ready, pour it into the saucepan with the oat mixture and whisk until fully incorporated.
8. Remove the saucepan from heat and let it sit for a minute to allow the flavors to meld.
9. Strain the mixture through a fine-mesh sieve to remove any lumps or oat bits.
10. Pour the Ecuadorian Quaker Coffee into a coffee cup.
11. Top generously with whipped cream and sprinkle some cocoa powder for added indulgence.
12. Serve immediately and enjoy the delightful fusion of oats, coffee, and aromatic spices.

Note: Feel free to adjust the sweetness and consistency according to your preference. You can also add a dash of nutmeg or a pinch of chili powder for an extra kick of flavor. Savor this exquisite Ecuadorian Quaker Coffee and let it transport you to the vibrant streets of Quito, where coffee is not just a beverage but a cultural phenomenon.

# South African Gemmer Koffie

**Ingredient List:**
- Freshly brewed coffee - 8 ounces (240 ml)
- Milk - 4 ounces (120 ml)
- Brown sugar - 2 tablespoons (30 grams)
- Ginger powder - 1 teaspoon (5 grams)
- Ground cinnamon - 1/4 teaspoon (1 gram)
- Nutmeg - a pinch
- Whipped cream - for garnish
- Ground cinnamon - for garnish

**Preparation time**: 10 minutes
**Portion Information**: Makes 2 servings
**Equipment Tips:**
- Coffee maker or French press for brewing coffee
- Measuring cups and spoons
- Small saucepan
- Whisk or spoon for stirring
- Coffee mugs

**Instructions:**
1. Brew 8 ounces (240 ml) of coffee using your preferred method. Ensure it is strong and aromatic, as it will provide the base for our Gemmer Koffie.
2. In a small saucepan, heat 4 ounces (120 ml) of milk over medium-low heat until hot, but not boiling. Stir occasionally to prevent scorching.
3. Add 2 tablespoons (30 grams) of brown sugar to the hot milk. Stir until the sugar has completely dissolved.
4. Sprinkle 1 teaspoon (5 grams) of ginger powder, 1/4 teaspoon (1 gram) of ground cinnamon, and a pinch of nutmeg into the milk. Whisk or stir vigorously to combine all the ingredients and infuse the flavors.
5. Reduce the heat to low and continue simmering the milk mixture for about 5 minutes, allowing the spices to meld with the milk and sugar.
6. While your milk mixture simmers, divide the freshly brewed coffee equally between two coffee mugs.
7. Once the milk mixture has simmered for 5 minutes, remove it from the heat.
8. Carefully pour half of the spiced milk into each coffee mug, over the brewed coffee. Use a spoon to gently mix the two together, creating a delightful blend of flavors.
9. If desired, top each Gemmer Koffie with a dollop of whipped cream and a sprinkle of ground cinnamon.
10. Serve immediately and enjoy the warm, aromatic South African Gemmer Koffie.

# Canadian Maple Latte

**Ingredient List:**
- 2 ounces (60 ml) espresso
- 8 ounces (240 ml) milk
- 1 tablespoon (15 ml) Canadian maple syrup
- 1/4 teaspoon (1.25 ml) vanilla extract
- 1/4 teaspoon (1.25 ml) ground cinnamon

**Preparation time**: 10 minutes
**Portion Information**: Makes 1 serving
**Equipment Tips:** Use an espresso machine for brewing espresso. A milk frother or steam wand will be handy for frothing the milk. If not available, a small saucepan and a whisk can be used.

**Instructions:**
1. Start by brewing 2 ounces (60 ml) of espresso. The rich and robust flavor of espresso is a crucial element in our Canadian Maple Latte.
2. While the espresso is brewing, pour 8 ounces (240 ml) of milk into a small frothing pitcher or saucepan. If using a saucepan, place it over low heat.
3. Froth the milk using a milk frother or steam wand. If using a saucepan, heat the milk over low heat and whisk vigorously until it becomes frothy. Frothing the milk will create a creamy texture in our latte.
4. Once the milk is frothy, remove it from the heat or stop frothing. Set it aside momentarily.
5. In a separate small bowl, combine 1 tablespoon (15 ml) of Canadian maple syrup, 1/4 teaspoon (1.25 ml) of vanilla extract, and 1/4 teaspoon (1.25 ml) of ground cinnamon. Mixing these ingredients together will bring a delightful aroma and sweetness to our latte.
6. Pour the brewed espresso into a serving cup or mug.
7. Slowly pour the frothed milk into the cup, allowing it to mix with the espresso. The combination of espresso and frothy milk creates the foundation of our latte.
8. Drizzle the maple syrup mixture over the top of the latte. The maple syrup adds a distinct Canadian touch and enhances the overall flavor profile.
9. If desired, sprinkle a pinch of ground cinnamon on top for an extra touch of warmth and spice.
10. Stir gently to combine all the flavors in our Canadian Maple Latte.
11. Savor the moment as you indulge in the velvety texture and enticing blend of espresso, milk, maple syrup, and cinnamon. This latte embodies the essence of culinary artistry with its harmonious interplay of flavors.

# Chapter 8:
# Iced Coffee Delights

Welcome to Chapter 8 of our coffee journey, where we explore the refreshing and invigorating world of iced coffee delights. In this chapter, we present 10+ tantalizing recipes that will awaken your taste buds and transport you to different corners of the globe. From the exotic Brazilian Caipirinha Coffee to the creamy Spanish Horchata Iced Coffee, each recipe offers a unique twist on the beloved iced coffee. Whether you crave the rich flavors of Thai Rose iced coffee or the tropical goodness of Hawaiian Pineapple Iced Coffee, this chapter has something to satisfy every coffee lover's craving. So grab your favorite glass and get ready to indulge in the frosty goodness of these delicious concoctions. Let's embark on this delightful journey of iced coffee together!

# Brazilian Caipirinha Coffee

**Ingredient List:**
- 2 ounces (60 ml) cachaça
- 1 ounce (30 ml) freshly squeezed lime juice
- 1 teaspoon (5 grams) white sugar
- 4 ounces (120 ml) freshly brewed coffee
- Fresh mint leaves for garnish

**Preparation time:** 10 minutes
**Portion Information:** This recipe makes 1 serving.
**Equipment Tips:**
- Cocktail shaker
- Muddler or wooden spoon
- Cocktail glass
- Strainer

**Instructions:**
1. In a cocktail shaker, combine the cachaça, lime juice, and sugar.
2. Use a muddler or the back of a wooden spoon to gently muddle the ingredients together, releasing the lime juice and incorporating the sugar.
3. Add ice cubes to the cocktail shaker, close it tightly, and shake vigorously for about 15 seconds to chill the mixture.
4. Place a strainer over a cocktail glass and strain the mixture into the glass, leaving the ice behind in the shaker.
5. Slowly pour the freshly brewed coffee into the glass, allowing it to cascade over the back of a spoon to create a layered effect.
6. Garnish with fresh mint leaves for a touch of elegance.
7. Serve immediately and enjoy the bold and refreshing flavors of the Brazilian Caipirinha Coffee.

Remember to drink responsibly and savor the moment. Cheers!

# Spanish Horchata Iced Coffee

**Ingredient List:**

- 1 cup (237 ml) almond milk
- 1/4 cup (59 ml) condensed milk
- 2 tablespoons (28 g) sugar
- 1/4 teaspoon (1.2 g) cinnamon powder
- 1/4 teaspoon (1.2 g) vanilla extract
- 1 cup (237 ml) brewed coffee, chilled
- Ice cubes
- Ground cinnamon, for garnish

**Preparation time:** 10 minutes

**Portion Information:** Makes 2 servings

**Equipment Tips:** Use a blender to combine the ingredients smoothly and a tall glass to serve the iced coffee beautifully.

**Instructions:**

1. In a blender, combine almond milk, condensed milk, sugar, cinnamon powder, and vanilla extract. Blend until all the ingredients are well-combined and the mixture becomes creamy.
2. Pour the chilled brewed coffee into the blender and blend it with the creamy mixture for a few seconds until it is fully incorporated.
3. Fill two tall glasses halfway with ice cubes.
4. Pour the horchata iced coffee mixture into the glasses over the ice cubes, dividing it equally between the two glasses.
5. Stir gently to mix the flavors and ensure the coffee and horchata are well-blended.
6. Sprinkle a pinch of ground cinnamon on top of each glass for an added touch of flavor and aesthetics.
7. Serve immediately and enjoy the refreshing Spanish Horchata Iced Coffee!

# German Eiskaffee

**Ingredient List:**
- 2 cups (480 ml) brewed coffee, cooled
- 4 scoops vanilla ice cream
- 1 tablespoon (15 ml) chocolate syrup
- Whipped cream, for garnish
- Chocolate shavings, for garnish

**Preparation time**: 10 minutes
**Portion Information:** Makes 2 servings
**Equipment Tips:**
- Brew fresh coffee and let it cool before starting.
- Use a blender to mix the ingredients smoothl

**Instructions:**
1. Start by preparing 2 cups of freshly brewed coffee and allow it to cool completely. You can speed up the cooling process by placing it in the refrigerator for a few minutes.
2. Once the coffee has cooled, add it to a blender along with 4 scoops of vanilla ice cream. This is where the magic begins! The contrasting temperatures of the chilled coffee and the creamy ice cream will result in a delightful texture and taste.
3. Blend the coffee and ice cream together until they are fully combined, creating a velvety and frothy mixture.
4. To enhance the flavor and add a touch of indulgence, drizzle 1 tablespoon of chocolate syrup into the blender. The rich chocolatey goodness will elevate the Eiskaffee experience to a whole new level.
5. Blend the mixture again briefly, just enough to incorporate the chocolate syrup, creating a beautifully marbled effect.
6. Once the Eiskaffee is ready, pour it into two tall glasses, leaving a small space at the top for garnishes.
7. Now it's time to add the finishing touches to this culinary masterpiece. Top each glass with a generous amount of whipped cream, creating a fluffy cloud that floats atop the coffee.
8. For an elegant touch, sprinkle some chocolate shavings over the whipped cream. These delicate curls will not only add visual appeal but will also provide irresistible chocolaty bursts in every sip.
9. Serve immediately, and savor the moment as you indulge in the creamy, caffeinated delight of German Eiskaffee.

# Thai Coconut Iced Coffee

**Ingredient List:**
- 2 ounces (60 ml) of strong coffee
- 2 tablespoons (30 ml) of condensed milk
- 2 tablespoons (30 ml) of coconut milk
- 1 teaspoon (5 ml) of vanilla extract
- Ice cubes
- Coconut flakes (optional, for garnish)

**Preparation time**: 10 minutes

**Portion Information**: This recipe makes 1 serving.

**Equipment Tips:**
- Use a coffee maker or a French press to make strong coffee.
- A blender or cocktail shaker will help you achieve a smooth and frothy texture.
- A tall glass or Mason jar can make your presentation more appealing.

**Instructions:**
1. Brew a strong coffee using your preferred method. Allow it to cool to room temperature.
2. In a blender or cocktail shaker, combine the cooled coffee, condensed milk, coconut milk, and vanilla extract.
3. Mix or shake vigorously until well combined and frothy.
4. Fill a glass with ice cubes, leaving some space at the top.
5. Pour the coffee mixture over the ice, making sure to include all the frothy goodness.
6. Stir gently to combine the flavors.
7. If desired, sprinkle some coconut flakes on top to enhance the tropical vibe.
8. Serve your Thai Coconut Iced Coffee immediately and enjoy the perfect balance of coffee, sweetness, and creaminess.

Note: If you prefer a stronger coconut flavor, you can increase the amount of coconut milk. Additionally, you can adjust the sweetness by adding more or less condensed milk to suit your taste. Experiment and have fun creating your signature Thai Coconut Iced Coffee!

# Mexican Chocolate Iced Coffee

**Ingredient List:**
- 2 oz (57 gr) Mexican chocolate
- 1 cup (240 ml) strong brewed coffee, chilled
- 1 cup (240 ml) milk
- 2 tbsp (30 ml) sweetened condensed milk
- 1 tsp (5 ml) vanilla extract
- 1 cup (240 ml) ice cubes
- Whipped cream, for topping
- Ground cinnamon, for garnish

**Preparation time:** 10 minutes
**Portion Information:** Makes 2 servings
**Equipment Tips:**
- Blender
- Saucepan
- Whisk

**Instructions:**
1. Start by melting the Mexican chocolate. Break the chocolate into small pieces and place it in a microwave-safe bowl. Heat it in the microwave for 30-second intervals, stirring in between, until fully melted. Alternatively, you can melt the chocolate in a small saucepan over low heat, stirring constantly until smooth.
2. In a blender, combine the chilled brewed coffee, milk, sweetened condensed milk, melted Mexican chocolate, vanilla extract, and ice cubes. Blend on high speed until all the ingredients are well combined and the mixture is frothy.
3. Take out two glasses and pour the Mexican chocolate iced coffee mixture evenly into each glass.
4. Top each glass with a generous dollop of whipped cream.
5. Finish off by sprinkling a pinch of ground cinnamon on top of the whipped cream for a delightful aroma and added flavor.
6. Serve immediately and enjoy your indulgent Mexican Chocolate Iced Coffee!

# Hawaiian Pineapple Iced Coffee

**Ingredient List:**

- 2 ounces (60 ml) freshly brewed coffee
- 1 ounce (30 ml) pineapple juice
- 1 ounce (30 ml) coconut milk
- 1 tablespoon (15 ml) honey
- 1 cup (250 ml) ice
- Pineapple slices, for garnish

**Preparation time:** 10 minutes

**Portion Information:** This recipe serves 1 portion.

**Equipment Tips:**

- Coffee maker or espresso machine
- Mixing glass or shaker
- Glassware for serving
- Blender or immersion blender (optional)

**Instructions:**

1. Prepare your coffee by brewing it according to your coffee maker's instructions. Alternatively, you can make a shot of espresso using an espresso machine. Allow the coffee to cool for a few minutes.
2. In a mixing glass or shaker, combine the freshly brewed coffee, pineapple juice, coconut milk, and honey. Stir or shake well to ensure everything is thoroughly mixed.
3. If you prefer a smoother texture, you can transfer the mixture to a blender or use an immersion blender to blend it for a few seconds.
4. Fill a glass with ice and pour the mixture over it, making sure to strain out any remaining bits of pineapple or coconut milk.
5. Garnish with a pineapple slice for an extra touch of tropical paradise.
6. Serve immediately and enjoy the refreshing taste of Hawaiian Pineapple Iced Coffee. Sip slowly to fully savor the flavors that blend harmoniously together.

# Australian Iced Caramel Latte

**Ingredient List:**
- 2 shots of espresso (60ml, 2 fl oz)
- 2 tablespoons of caramel syrup (30ml, 1 fl oz)
- 1 cup of milk (240ml, 8 fl oz)
- 1 tablespoon of sugar (12g)
- Ice cubes

**Preparation time**: 10 minutes
**Portion Information:** Makes 1 serving
**Equipment Tips:** It is recommended to use an espresso machine or a stovetop espresso maker, a milk frother or steam wand, a glass for serving, and a spoon for stirring.

**Instructions:**
1. Brew the 2 shots of espresso using an espresso machine or a stovetop espresso maker, and pour it into a glass.
2. Add the caramel syrup to the glass and stir well to combine it with the espresso.
3. In a separate container, heat the milk until hot but not boiling. You can use a milk frother or steam wand to froth the milk if desired.
4. Pour the hot milk over the caramel espresso mixture in the glass, holding back the foam with a spoon to create layers.
5. Add the sugar to the glass and stir until the sugar has dissolved.
6. Fill the glass with ice cubes, leaving some space at the top for the foam.
7. Gently scoop the milk foam onto the top of the glass, creating a layer of froth.
8. Optionally, drizzle some additional caramel syrup on top for added sweetness and decoration.
9. Serve immediately and enjoy the captivating blend of caramel, espresso, and creamy milk in this refreshing Australian Iced Caramel Latte. Sit back, sip, and savor the artistry of this culinary delight.

# Australian Iced Mocha

**Ingredient List:**
- Espresso - 2 shots (60 ml / 2 oz)
- Chocolate syrup - 2 tablespoons (30 ml / 1 oz)
- Milk - 1 cup (240 ml / 8 oz)
- Ice cubes - 1 cup (240 ml / 8 oz)
- Whipped cream - for garnish
- Cocoa powder - for garnish

**Preparation time**: 10 minutes
**Portion Information:** Makes 1 serving
**Equipment Tips:**
- Espresso machine or coffee maker
- Blender
- Tall glass or mason jar
- Whisk or electric mixer (for homemade whipped cream)

**Instructions:**
1. Start by preparing your espresso. If you have an espresso machine, use it to brew 2 shots of espresso. If not, brew a strong cup of coffee using your coffee maker and set it aside to cool.
2. In a blender, combine the chocolate syrup, milk, and ice cubes. Blend on high speed until the mixture is smooth and frothy.
3. Take a tall glass or mason jar and pour the blended mixture into it, filling it about halfway.
4. Slowly pour in the prepared espresso shots, allowing it to mix with the blended mixture. You should see a beautiful swirl forming in the glass.
5. Give it a gentle stir to fully incorporate the espresso into the mixture.
6. Top the glass with a swirl of whipped cream. You can either use store-bought whipped cream or make your own by whisking or using an electric mixer to beat heavy cream and a bit of sugar until stiff peaks form.
7. Finish off with a sprinkle of cocoa powder on top of the whipped cream for an elegant touch.
8. Serve immediately and enjoy the heavenly combination of rich chocolate, bold coffee, and creamy milk in each sip.

# Vietnamese Iced Coffee

**Ingredient List:**
- 2 tablespoons (30 ml) ground Vietnamese coffee
- 6 ounces (180 ml) hot water
- 2 tablespoons (30 ml) sweetened condensed milk
- Ice cubes

**Preparation time**: 10 minutes
**Portion Information:** Makes 1 serving
**Equipment Tips:**
- French press or Vietnamese coffee filter
- Heat-resistant glass or cup
- Stirrer or long-handled spoon

Detailed instructions for preparation and cooking:
1. Start by preparing your coffee. If using a French press, add the ground Vietnamese coffee to the bottom of the press. If using a Vietnamese coffee filter, add the coffee to the filter chamber.
2. Pour hot water, about 6 ounces (180 ml), over the coffee grounds. Allow the coffee to steep for about 4-5 minutes. For a stronger brew, increase the steeping time to 6-7 minutes.
3. While the coffee is steeping, take a heat-resistant glass or cup and pour the sweetened condensed milk into it.
4. Once the steeping time is complete, slowly press down the plunger on the French press or place the lid with the filter on top of the coffee cup to strain the coffee.
5. Pour the freshly brewed coffee over the sweetened condensed milk. The milk will gradually dissolve, creating a lovely combination of flavors.
6. Stir the mixture gently until the condensed milk is fully incorporated into the coffee. This will create a smooth and creamy texture.
7. Fill a tall glass with ice cubes and pour the Vietnamese coffee over the ice.
8. Give it another gentle stir to ensure the coffee and ice are well combined.
9. Serve immediately and enjoy the refreshing and invigorating flavors of Vietnamese Iced Coffee!

# Thai Iced Coffee

**Ingredient List:**
- 4 ounces (120 ml) strong brewed coffee
- 2 tablespoons (30 ml) condensed milk
- 1 cup (240 ml) ice cubes

**Preparation time:** 5 minutes
**Portion Information:** Makes 1 serving
**Equipment Tips:** For brewing the coffee, use a French press or a drip coffee maker. A blender or cocktail shaker will be handy for mixing the ingredients.

Detailed instructions for preparation and cooking:
1. Start by brewing a strong cup of coffee. You can use 4 ounces (120 ml) of any coffee you prefer. For an authentic Thai taste, using dark-roast coffee is recommended.
2. Pour the coffee into a heatproof container and let it cool for a few minutes. It's important to let it cool down to avoid melting the ice too quickly.
3. Once the coffee has cooled, add 2 tablespoons (30 ml) of condensed milk. Adjust the amount according to your preference for sweetness. The condensed milk will provide a creamy and sweet flavor to the iced coffee.
4. Stir the coffee and condensed milk together until well combined. You can use a spoon, whisk, or even a frother to mix them thoroughly.
5. Fill a glass with 1 cup (240 ml) of ice cubes. The amount of ice can be adjusted based on your preference for a stronger or milder coffee flavor.
6. Slowly pour the coffee mixture over the ice. The ice will cool down the coffee and create a refreshing drink.
7. Give the Thai Iced Coffee a gentle stir to ensure that the flavors are evenly distributed and the coffee is thoroughly chilled.
8. Serve immediately and enjoy the delightful taste of Thai Iced Coffee. Appreciate the harmonious balance between the strong coffee and the creamy sweetness from the condensed milk.

# British Iced Mocha

**Ingredient List:**
- 2 shots of espresso (60 ml)
- 1 cup of cold milk (240 ml)
- 2 tablespoons of chocolate syrup (30 ml)
- 1 tablespoon of sugar (15 gr)
- Ice cubes

**Preparation time:** 10 minutes
**Portion Information:** 1 serving
**Equipment Tips:**
- Espresso machine or coffee maker
- Milk frother or whisk
- Tall glass or mason jar for serving
- Stirrer or long spoon

**Instructions:**
1. Brew 2 shots of espresso using an espresso machine or coffee maker. Pour the hot espresso into a tall glass and let it cool for a few minutes.
2. While the espresso is cooling, froth the milk using a milk frother or whisk until it becomes creamy and slightly thick. Set aside.
3. Add chocolate syrup and sugar to the cooled espresso in the glass. Stir well until the syrup and sugar are fully dissolved.
4. Fill the glass with ice cubes, leaving some space at the top.
5. Slowly pour the frothed milk over the ice cubes, allowing it to mix with the espresso and chocolate syrup.
6. Gently stir the mixture with a stirrer or long spoon to combine all the flavors.
7. Serve immediately, garnishing with a drizzle of chocolate syrup if desired.

# Thai Thai Iced Tea Coffee

**Ingredient List:**
- 4 ounces (120 ml) of Thai tea leaves
- 4 cups (960 ml) of water
- 4 ounces (120 ml) of sweetened condensed milk
- 4 ounces (120 ml) of evaporated milk
- 2 cups (480 ml) of strong brewed coffee, chilled
- Ice cubes

**Preparation time**: 1 hour
**Portion Information**: This recipe serves 4 portions.
**Equipment Tips:**
- Large pot
- Strainer
- Pitcher
- Mixing spoon
- Glasses or mugs

**Instructions:**
1. In a large pot, bring the water to a boil.
2. Add the Thai tea leaves to the boiling water and let it steep for 5 minutes. Stir occasionally to extract the flavors.
3. After 5 minutes, strain the brewed tea into a pitcher. Discard the tea leaves.
4. Add the sweetened condensed milk and evaporated milk to the pitcher containing the brewed Thai tea. Stir well until the milk is fully incorporated.
5. Chill the Thai tea mixture in the refrigerator for at least 30 minutes.
6. In the meantime, prepare the strong brewed coffee using your preferred method. Allow it to cool completely before using.
7. Once both the Thai tea mixture and the coffee are chilled, take out the pitcher from the refrigerator and stir the mixture gently.
8. Fill four glasses or mugs with ice cubes.
9. Pour equal amounts of the Thai tea mixture over the ice in each glass, filling each glass about halfway.
10. Slowly pour the chilled brewed coffee over the Thai tea mixture in each glass until the glass is almost full.
11. Stir gently to combine the layers of Thai tea and coffee.
12. Serve immediately and enjoy the delightful fusion of Thai Thai Iced Tea Coffee.

# BONUS:
# How to Accompany Coffee

As we have already discussed earlier, coffee is a versatile and delightful beverage that can be enjoyed on its own. However, there are numerous ways to enhance the coffee-drinking experience by pairing it with various foods and treats. In this chapter, we will explore some creative and delightful options for accompanying your delicious cup of joe.

1. Biscotti: These crunchy Italian cookies are a classic companion to coffee. Their firm texture and subtle sweetness provide the perfect contrast to the smooth taste of a well-brewed cup. You can even experiment with different flavors like almond, chocolate, or even citrus-infused biscotti. Dunking these cookies into your coffee allows them to soften just enough to melt in your mouth while still maintaining their integrity. It's a delightful ritual that adds an extra layer of enjoyment to your coffee break.
2. Cheese and Crackers: While this may seem like an unconventional pairing at first, the combination of creamy cheese and crispy crackers can complement the complex flavors of coffee surprisingly well. Soft, mild cheeses like Brie or Camembert provide a rich and creamy element that blends beautifully with the bitterness of coffee. The crunch of the crackers adds a satisfying textural contrast, creating a harmonious balance of flavors with your cup of coffee.
3. Fresh Fruit: Incorporating fresh fruit into your coffee experience can introduce new dimensions of taste and aroma. Berries such as strawberries, blueberries, or raspberries make particularly wonderful companions to coffee. Their natural sweetness and vibrant

colors add a refreshing touch to your coffee break. You can enjoy them as they are or even try lightly macerating them in a bit of sugar to release their juices and intensify their flavors.
4. Dark Chocolate: For all the chocolate lovers out there, pairing rich, high-quality dark chocolate with your coffee is an indulgent treat. The deep and slightly bitter notes of dark chocolate can harmonize exquisitely with the robust flavors of coffee. Break off a small piece of chocolate and let it melt on your tongue as you savor a sip of your favorite brew. The combination of these two decadent flavors will transport you to a realm of pure delight.
5. Nuts: Whether enjoyed on their own or as a part of granola or trail mix, nuts can bring a delightful crunch and earthy flavor to your coffee experience. Options such as almonds, pecans, or hazelnuts can amplify the nutty undertones in coffee, creating a harmonious and satisfying combination. You can even try toasting them lightly before enjoying them with your cup of coffee for an added layer of aromatic delight.
6. Spiced Treats: Embrace the warm and cozy flavors of fall by pairing your coffee with spiced treats. Options like cinnamon rolls, pumpkin bread, or gingerbread cookies add a touch of seasonal indulgence to your coffee break. The comforting spices in these treats elevate the flavors of your coffee, creating a delightful synergy that will leave you feeling warm and content.

As the traveler finishes their last bite and sips the remnants of their coffee, they feel a sense of belonging and contentment. They thank Hans for the delightful experience and promise to return someday. With a newfound appreciation for the art of pairing spiced treats with coffee, the traveler embarks on their journey, carrying the warmth of Hans' bakery in their heart.

As you explore the world of coffee pairings, remember that taste is subjective, and everyone has their own preferences. Don't be afraid to experiment and find your unique combinations that truly elevate your coffee experience. With the multitude of flavors and textures available, there are endless possibilities for exploring and enhancing your coffee breaks. So go ahead, grab your favorite snack or treat, and savor every sip alongside a delightful companion to your cup of joe.

# Conclusion

Our journey through the rich and aromatic world of coffee draws to a close. As we reach the end of this delightful exploration, I invite you to savor this moment and reflect on the wonders and joys that coffee has brought into your life. Throughout the pages of this book, we've delved into the history, the art, and the science of coffee, discovering its cultural significance and its myriad ways of bringing people together. We've explored the diverse coffee brewing methods, from the comforting French press to the mesmerizing siphon, and we've uncovered the secrets to creating the perfect cup.

In this conclusion, we'll not only recap the highlights of our coffee journey but also look forward to the continued adventure that awaits you as a coffee enthusiast. Coffee is more than a beverage; it's a lifestyle, a passion, and a means of connecting with people and cultures from around the world. As you turn the final page, may you carry with you the knowledge, the appreciation, and the love for coffee that you've cultivated throughout this journey.

**Reflecting on Our Coffee Odyssey**

The first chapter of our book delved into the historical origins of coffee, tracing its path from the ancient coffeehouses of Yemen to the bustling coffee shops of today. Coffee's journey has been as diverse and exciting as the flavors it offers, and it's a testament to the power of a single beverage to transcend time and culture.

We explored the art of coffee in great depth, from the careful selection of beans to the precision of brewing methods. The world of coffee is a canvas waiting for your creative touch, whether you're experimenting with different grind sizes, exploring various extraction times, or immersing yourself in the delicate art of latte art.

Throughout this book, we've delved into the characteristics of coffee, from the flavors and aromas that fill your senses to the origins that shape the unique personality of each cup. You've come to understand that coffee is not just a drink; it's an experience that engages your senses and your soul.

Our journey took us through the intricate world of brewing methods, from the simplicity of the French press to the elegance of the siphon. Each method brought its unique charm and flavor profile, offering you the chance to discover new dimensions of your coffee palate.

As you close this book, you carry with you a treasure trove of knowledge about coffee, its history, its art, and its science. You've become a coffee enthusiast, a connoisseur, and a true aficionado. Your senses are now attuned to the subtle nuances of coffee, and you can discern the delicate balance of flavors in each cup you brew.

**Embrace the Joy of Experimentation**

The world of coffee is a vast and exciting playground, and as a coffee enthusiast, you have the privilege of exploring it to your heart's content. This is the beauty of coffee; it's not just a drink but a journey of discovery. Every cup is an opportunity to experiment and create something uniquely yours.

As you venture into the world of coffee, I encourage you to embrace the joy of experimentation. The perfect cup of coffee is a highly personal and ever-evolving pursuit. It's about finding what suits your taste buds, your mood, and the occasion. You might find solace in the simplicity of a well-brewed French press or the precision of a pour-over method. You might be drawn to the intensity of espresso or the mesmerizing vacuum brewing of the siphon.

Experiment with grind sizes, water temperatures, and brew times. Taste the subtle variations in flavor that each adjustment brings. Revel in the alchemy of brewing, where small changes can lead to significant transformations in your cup.

**Share the Coffee Experience**

As a coffee enthusiast, you are now part of a global community bound by a common love for this extraordinary beverage. Coffee transcends borders, languages, and cultures, and it has the power to connect people in ways that few other things can.

So, don't keep this journey to yourself. Share the joy of coffee with friends and family. Brew a pot of your favorite coffee, and invite them to join you in a delightful moment of togetherness. Share stories, laughter, and conversations, all over the comforting aroma of freshly brewed coffee. Let coffee be the catalyst for new connections and memorable experiences.

In the age of coffee shops and specialty coffee culture, you have the opportunity to explore the world's coffee offerings. Sample different beans, roasts, and brewing methods, and share your discoveries with others. Recommend a coffee shop to a friend, introduce them to a new blend, or simply enjoy a cup together.

Coffee is not just a beverage; it's a shared experience. It's the connection you make over a cup of coffee, the stories you tell, and the memories you create. It's the warmth that spreads from your fingertips to your heart when you cradle a steaming mug.

The Adventure Continues

As you close this book and embark on your continued journey with coffee, remember that the adventure has just begun.

Made in United States
Troutdale, OR
12/12/2023